REGENTS RESTORATION DRAMA SERIES

General Editor: John Loftis

THE VIRTUOSO

THOMAS SHADWELL, 1642?-1692.

The Virtuoso

Edited by

MARJORIE HOPE NICOLSON
and
DAVID STUART RODES

UNIVERSITY OF NEBRASKA PRESS · LINCOLN

First Bison Book printing March, 1966

Most recent printing shown by first digit below:

2   3   4   5   6   7   8   9   10

MANUFACTURED IN THE UNITED STATES OF AMERICA

Regents Restoration Drama Series

The Regents Restoration Drama Series, similar in objectives and format to the Regents Renaissance Drama Series, will provide soundly edited texts, in modern spelling, of the more significant English plays of the late seventeenth and early eighteenth centuries. The word "Restoration" is here used ambiguously and must be explained. If to the historian it refers to the period between 1660 and 1685 (or 1688), it has long been used by the student of drama in default of a more precise word to refer to plays belonging to the dramatic tradition established in the 1660's, weakening after 1700, and displaced in the 1730's. It is in this extended sense—imprecise though justified by academic custom—that the word is used in this series, which will include plays first produced between 1660 and 1737. Although these limiting dates are determined by political events, the return of Charles II (and the removal of prohibitions against the operation of theaters) and the passage of Walpole's Stage Licensing Act, they enclose a period of dramatic history having a coherence of its own in the establishment, development, and disintegration of a tradition.

Each text in the series is based on a fresh collation of the seventeenth- and eighteenth-century editions that might be presumed to have authority. The textual notes, which appear above the rule at the bottom of each page, record all substantive departures from the edition used as the copy-text. Variant substantive readings among contemporary editions are listed there as well. Editions later than the eighteenth century are referred to in the textual notes only when an emendation originating in some one of them is received into the text. Variants of accidentals (spelling, punctuation, capitalization) are not recorded in the notes. Contracted forms of characters' names are silently expanded in speech prefixes and stage directions, and, in the case of speech prefixes, are regularized. Additions to the stage directions of the copy-text are enclosed in brackets. Stage directions such as "within" or "aside" are enclosed in parentheses when they occur in the copy-text.

Spelling has been modernized along consciously conservative lines, but within the limits of a modernized text the linguistic quality of the original has been carefully preserved. Punctuation has been brought into accord with modern practices. The objective has been to achieve a balance between the generally light pointing of the old editions, and a system of punctuation which, without overloading the text with exclamation marks, semicolons, and dashes, will make the often loosely flowing verse and prose of the original syntactically intelligible to the modern reader. Dashes are regularly used only to indicate interrupted speeches, or shifts of address within a single speech.

Explanatory notes, chiefly concerned with glossing obsolete words and phrases, are printed below the textual notes at the bottom of each page. References to stage directions in the notes follow the admirable system of the Revels editions, whereby stage directions are keyed, decimally, to the line of the text before or after which they occur. Thus, a note on 0.2 has reference to the second line of the stage direction at the beginning of the scene in question. A note on 115.1 has reference to the first line of the stage direction following line 115 of the text of the relevant scene. Speech prefixes, and any stage directions attached to them, are keyed to the first line of accompanying dialogue.

JOHN LOFTIS

Stanford University

Contents

Abbreviations

Borgman	Albert S. Borgman. *Thomas Shadwell, His Life and Comedies*. New York, 1928.
Lloyd	Claude Lloyd. "Shadwell and the Virtuosi," *PMLA*, XLIV (1929), 472–494.
OED	*Oxford English Dictionary*
om.	omitted
Pepys	*The Diary of Samuel Pepys*. Edited with additions by Henry B. Wheatley. 9 vols. London, Bell, 1897.
PMLA	*Publications of the Modern Language Association of America*
Phil. Trans.	*Philosophical Transactions* [of the Royal Society]*: giving some Accompt of the Present Undertakings, Studies, and Labours of the Ingenious in Many Considerable Parts of the World*. Each volume is dated separately for the years it covers.
Q1	The first edition, a quarto of 1676
Q2	The second edition, a quarto of 1676
Q3	The third edition, a quarto of 1691
S.D.	Stage direction
S.P.	Speech prefix
Summers	*The Complete Works of Thomas Shadwell*. Edited by Montague Summers. 4 vols. London, 1927.

Introduction

TEXTUAL AND THEATRICAL HISTORY

Two editions of *The Virtuoso* appeared in 1676,[1] both "Printed by
T[homas] *N*[ewcombe] for *Henry Herringman*." Some doubt persists
about the order of priority. As the copy-text for the present edition
we have used the one noted in the Huntington Library as "probably
1st ed." It is so considered by Thomas James Wise.[2] This edition is
collated as follows:

Quarto; pp. vii + 100 + [2].
Signature A to N (13 sheets, each four leaves) and O (3 leaves).

Its title page reads as follows:

THE/ VIRTUOSO./ A/ COMEDY,/ Acted at the/ DUKE'S
THEATRE./ [rule]/ Written by/ *THOMAS SHADWELL.*/
[rule]/ Licensed *May* 31. 1676./ *ROGER L'ESTRANGE.*/ [rule]/
LONDON,/ Printed by *T. N.* for *Henry Herringman*, at the *Anchor*/
in the Lower Walk of the *New Exchange*. 1676.

The second edition is collated as follows:

Quarto; pp. vi + 88 + [2].
Signature A to M (12 sheets, each 4 leaves). (Signature B2 is
signed B3.)

In this edition pages 41 and 82 are numbered 42 and 72 respectively.
The title reads as the first except for an inverted "s" in "Duke's"
in the sixth line and various other minor typographical variations.[3]

[1] The Stationers entry is given "1mo Junii 1676." The Term Catalogue
lists the play at Michaelmas (Fall Term), 1676.

[2] *The Ashley Library: A Catalogue of Printed Books, Manuscripts and Autograph
Letters Collected by Thomas James Wise* (London, 1922–1936), V, 3.
Pforzheimer accepts this order as do Woodward and McManaway. See
The Carl H. Pforzheimer Library: English Literature, 1475–1700 (New York,
1940), III, 907, no. 877; and *A Check List of English Plays, 1641–1700,*
compiled by Gertrude L. Woodward and James G. McManaway (Chicago,
1945), nos. 1102, 1103.

[3] The Pforzheimer Library has a copy of this edition, and it is described
in detail in that catalogue. Pforzheimer, III, 907, no. 877.

In 1691, perhaps in response to Shadwell's appointment as Poet Laureate,[4] a third edition of *The Virtuoso* was printed for *"Henry Herringman"* to be sold by *"Francis Saunders,* at the *Blue-Anchor* . . . and *James Knapton,* at the *Crown* . . . ." It is collated as follows:

Quarto; pp. vi + 62 + [2].
Signature A to H (8 sheets, each 4 leaves) and I (3 leaves).

These three editions, the only ones published during Shadwell's lifetime, form the basis for the present edition and will be designated respectively in the textual notes as Q1, Q2, and Q3. Collation revealed no major variations among these three relevant editions.

After Shadwell's death in 1692, seventeen of his plays were bound together in one volume which appeared with a new general title page in 1693. The 1691 edition of *The Virtuoso* was included as number four (instead of number eight, as chronologically it should have been in the sequence of Shadwell's dramatic works). A fourth edition of *The Virtuoso* was published in 1704. The plays gathered together in 1693 were published in a collected edition in 1720 with a dedication to George I written by Shadwell's son John.

The Virtuoso was produced by the Duke's Company at Dorset Garden in May, 1676. The Lord Chamberlain's Records lists a performance on May 25, 1676, which was attended by the King.[5] Anthony Leigh took the role of Sir Formal Trifle[6] and Nokes probably that of Sir Samuel Hearty.[7] The comedy was well received except,

4 The title page reads as follows: "Written By/ *THOMAS SHADWELL,* Laur."

5 "His Ma[ts] Bill from His Royall Highnesse Theatre. . . . May 25 at the Virtuoso . . . £10 . . . ." Quoted in Allardyce Nicoll, *A History of English Drama, 1660–1900* (Cambridge, 1955), I, 348.

6 John Downes, *Roscius Anglicanus, or, an Historical Review of the Stage from 1660 to 1706, A Fac-simile Reprint of the Rare Original of 1708, With an Historical Preface by Joseph Knight* (London, 1886), p. 41.

7 As Montague Summers (ed., *The Complete Works of Thomas Shadwell* [London, 1927], III, 99) and Albert S. Borgman (*Thomas Shadwell, His Life and Comedies* [New York, 1928], p. 31 n.) observe, in Mrs. Behn's *Sir Patient Fancy* (*The Works*, Summers ed., IV, 70), Sir Credulous says, "Very well, put me into this Basket, and cord me down, send for a couple of Porters, hoist me away with a Direction to an old Uncle of mine . . . and then whip slap-dash, as Nokes says in the Play, I'm gone, and who's the wiser?" Sir Samuel Hearty is brought onstage in a chest, and "whip slapdash" is one of his favorite expressions. Summers believes that Cave Underhill played Snarl, but we can find no evidence for this.

as Shadwell himself suggested in the Dedicatory Epistle, by "some women, and some men of feminine understandings, who like slight plays only . . ." (ll. 63–64). Of *The Libertine* and *The Virtuoso* Downes records that "they were both very well Acted, and got the Company great Reputation."[8] And Langbaine reports that "the University of Oxford, who may be allowed Competent Judges of Comedy, (especially of such Characters, as Sir *Nicholas Gimcrack*, and Sir *Formal Trifle*) applauded it: and as no Man ever undertook to discover the Frailties of such Pretenders to this kind of Knowledge, before Mr. *Shadwell*; so none since Mr. *Johnson's* Time, ever drew so many different Characters of Humours, and with such Success."[9]

The comedy was occasionally played for some years. It was advertised in the *London Gazette* of July 3–6, 1676.[10] As late as 1699 Gildon stated that this "Play . . . has always found Success,"[11] implying that it was still performed from time to time. The play was last acted professionally, so far as is known, at Lincoln's Inn Fields, March 31, 1705.[12]

Montague Summers considers that while all of the characters "are very well drawn . . . the three glories of the piece are Sir Samuel Hearty, old Snarl, and Sir Formal Trifle, and the greatest of these is Sir Formal."[13] Sir Formal, the sententious Ciceronian orator and

[8] Downes, p. 37.

[9] Gerard Langbaine, *An Account of the English Dramatick Poets* (Oxford, 1691), pp. 451–452.

[10] Quoted in Sybil Rosenfeld, "Dramatic Advertisements in the Burney Newspapers, 1660–1700," *PMLA*, LI (1936), 131.

[11] [Charles Gildon], *The Lives and Characters of the English Dramatick Poets . . . . First begun by Mr. Langbain, improv'd and continued down to this Time, by a Careful Hand* (London, 1699[?]), p. 178.

[12] John Genest, *Some Account of the English Stage* (Bath, 1832), II, 329. According to Genest, this performance was given as a benefit for Cave Underhill, and Summers (III, 99) and Borgman (p. 160 n.) believe that Underhill may have taken the part of Snarl.
The London Stage, 1660–1800 lists only two performances of *The Virtuoso* in the eighteenth century: this performance on March 31, 1705, and an earlier one, a benefit for Hodgson and Bowen, on September 25, 1700, both at Lincoln's Inn Fields. *The London Stage, 1660–1800, Part 2: 1700–1729*, ed. with a critical introduction by Emmett L. Avery (Carbondale, Ill., 1960), I, 4, 91.

[13] Summers, I, cxliii. The source of Sir Formal Trifle is traced to Sir Solemn Trifle in D'Avenant's *News From Plymouth* (*c.* 1635) by G. Blakemore Evans, "The Source of Shadwell's Character of Sir Formal Trifle in 'The Virtuoso,'" *Modern Language Review*, XXXV (1940), 211–214.

coxcomb, established a type that became proverbial. Shadwell himself referred to Sir Formal in two other plays, *A True Widow* and *The Woman Captain*.[14] Both Otway and Tate mention Sir Formal in their respective prefaces to *Don Carlos* (1676) and *Brutus of Alba* (1678). In *The Fool Turn'd Critick* (Nov., 1676) Thomas D'Urfey introduced a certain Sir Formal Ancient, an oratorical pedant; and in *The Adventures of Lindamira, A Lady of Quality* (1702) Tom Brown showed his heroine beset by the pedantic and priggish Sir Formal Trifle.

The other characters were not forgotten. In November of the year *The Virtuoso* was first performed, D'Urfey picked up some details from Sir Nicholas for his Sir Arthur Oldlove and from Snarl for Captain Tilbury, "an old fashioned blunt fellow," in *Madam Fickle*. And Congreve's Lady Plyant in *The Double-Dealer* was surely patterned after Lady Gimcrack, several of whose speeches Lady Plyant delivers almost verbatim.

Though we may agree with Pope that Sir Nicholas Gimcrack, the Virtuoso, "does not maintain his character with equal strength to the end,"[15] it is, of all the characterizations, this title figure who most powerfully impressed later writers. In addition to the use D'Urfey made of Sir Nicholas, there is Lawrence Maidwell's imitation of the Virtuoso type in *The Loving Enemies* (*c.* March, 1680), for which Shadwell himself furnished an epilogue. There is a passing suggestion of Shadwell's member of the Royal Society in the figure of Periwinkle, "a kind of silly Virtuoso," in Mrs. Centlivre's *A Bold Stroke for a Wife* (Feb., 1718), but much more in her earlier *The Basset Table* (Nov., 1705), particularly in the character of the little virtuosa, Valeria, "a Philosophical Girl," whose passion for collecting and for microscopical observation is affectionately treated by Mrs. Centlivre. Doctor Boliardo in Aphra Behn's *The Emperor of the Moon* (March, 1687) has many traits in common with Shadwell's scientist,[16] and Peter Pindar's Sir Joseph Banks, who boils fifteen hundred fleas to prove they will turn crimson like lobsters,[17] seems decidedly to be a

[14] Summers, III, 300, and IV, 72.

[15] Related by Joseph Spence, *Anecdotes, Observations, and Characters, of Books and Men*, ed. Samuel Weller Singer (2nd ed., London, 1858), p. 10.

[16] Doctor Boliardo is indeed a virtuoso in much the same sense as Gimcrack, though on the whole Mrs. Behn's sources were to be found in non-dramatic rather than dramatic literature. See Marjorie Nicolson, *Voyages to the Moon* (New York, 1948, paperback, 1960), pp. 88–93.

[17] "Sir Joseph Banks and the Boiled Fleas," [John Wolcot], *The Works of*

descendant of Sir Nicholas. That Sir Nicholas Gimcrack continued
to live may be most convincingly seen in Steele's description of his
will in *The Tatler* and in Swift's choice of experiments for the Grand
Academy of Lagado in the third book of *Gulliver's Travels.*[18]

SATIRE ON THE NEW SCIENCE

Although the characters Sir Formal Trifle, Sir Samuel Hearty,
Snarl, and especially Sir Nicholas Gimcrack undoubtedly had their
appeal and influence, there is little question that an important
reason for the enthusiastic reception of the comedy—and its chief
originality—lay in its satire on contemporary science. Shadwell's
was the most extensive treatment of this theme in drama since Ben
Jonson's *The Alchemist*. His satire was more immediate and specific
than Jonson's, since his light artillery was trained particularly upon
the Royal Society of London. Although this fact was pointed out by
Carson S. Duncan as early as 1913,[19] general attention was first
drawn to it by an article on *The Virtuoso*, published by Claude Lloyd
in 1929,[20] in which he showed the origin of nearly every phase of
Shadwell's scientific satire. Since Mr. Lloyd's article is readily

---

Peter Pindar, Esquire, 3 vols. (London, 1794), II, 393–397. In the same
volume see "Peter's Prophecy; or, the President and Poet; or, an Important
Epistle to Sir J. Banks, on the Approaching Election of a President of the
Royal Society," pp. 103–143; and "Sir Joseph Banks and the Emperor of
Morocco, A Tale," pp. 187–206.

[18] See below.

[19] Carson S. Duncan, *The New Science and English Literature in the Classical
Period* (Menasha, Wisconsin), 1913. This doctoral dissertation was really
the pioneer in what has become a popular field, Science and Literature.
Unfortunately Mr. Duncan, like many other doctoral candidates, published
his thesis at his own expense with a press that offered no promotional
facilities so that the result was tantamount to the book's having been
"privately printed." Montague Summers obviously did not know it when
he edited *The Virtuoso*. In his critical introduction he mentions the Royal
Society but says nothing about the origin of Gimcrack's experiments in
Phil. Trans.

[20] Mr. Lloyd analyzes all the scientific satire, with specific reference to
real experiments, particularly in *Phil. Trans.* and in Robert Hooke's
Micrographia, in which he says he found the greatest amount of material.
Since the time of his article, much more information on Hooke and other
experimental scientists has been made available in R. T. Gunther's
monumental *Early Science in Oxford* (Oxford, 1923–1945), five volumes of
which are devoted to *The Life and Works of Robert Hooke*.

available, I shall enter only occasionally into a comparison of Shadwell and his sources, but shall rather try to assist the Shadwell student by indicating what general aspects of the New Science seemed humorous to the Restoration audience. I must begin with what Shadwell could take for granted—some knowledge of the Royal Society.

To some extent at least the foundation of the Royal Society was an attempt on the part of followers of Francis Bacon to establish in England a sort of "Salomon's House," which he had described in the *New Atlantis*. Actually, however, the Royal Society, like Topsy, was never born but "just growed," preceded as it had been by various continental academies which had lived a shorter or longer period, but no one of which—unlike the Royal Society—was to continue to our day.[21] The Society was in large part a continuation of Gresham College, which had been established in the last years of the sixteenth century by the will of Sir Thomas Gresham, who had left his estate to the City of London, in trust for the citizens, as a place where adults might continue their education. Public lectures were given on various subjects, among which was Natural Philosophy or Natural History (the word "science" was seldom used in our modern sense in the seventeenth century). So close was the relationship between the earlier and the later organization that the Royal Society continued to be known by most people, including many of its members, as "Gresham College," or "the College." This will explain Lady Gimcrack's remark about Sir Nicholas: "The College indeed refus'd him. They envied him" (II.i.304).

Two other steps in the development of the Society merit passing attention. One involved a group of men interested in science, which may or may not have been "The Invisible College." The most famous today was Robert Boyle. Around 1645 they began to hold informal meetings in London. About 1648 several of them, including Boyle, moved to Oxford where they joined the Philosophical Society at Wadham College, under the wardenship of John Wilkins. Among the members were Sir William Petty, Seth Ward, Thomas Sprat, the future historian of the Society, and Christopher Wren, then known as anatomist and astronomer rather than as the architect who was to

21 There are a number of histories of the Royal Society. As a background for Restoration literature, the most interesting is Dorothy Stimson, *Scientists and Amateurs: A History of the Royal Society* (New York, 1948). On the "Invisible College," see her note, p. 37.

rebuild London from her ashes. At the time of the Restoration, with the change of political parties which affected the universities, there was a good deal of movement from the universities to London. At this period members of the various groups then resident in the city organized the Royal Society, which was chartered by Charles II in 1662, shortly after his own Restoration. Here gathered some one hundred persons, some of them scientists in our sense, but the majority merely amateurs—aristocrats and gentlemen of leisure, clergymen, men of letters, among them Cowley, Evelyn, and Dryden. These were the "Virtuosi," as they came popularly to be called and as they sometimes called themselves.

The term *virtuoso* had come into use earlier in the century,[22] originally applied to what we should call an "antiquarian," who interested himself in such antiquities as statues, inscriptions, coins. The word might be used for compliment or for disparagement, suggesting on the one hand a connoisseur, on the other a mere dabbler. Although Boyle used the term about men interested in science and, indeed, called his own treatise on science and religion *The Christian Virtuoso*, the most frequent popular application was to "collectors," usually in a pejorative sense. Sir Nicholas Gimcrack was a collector, and from the point of view of his nieces at least, of worthless objects. "One who has broken his brains about the nature of maggots, who has studied these twenty years to find out the several sorts of spiders, and never cares for understanding mankind" (I.ii.11–13). Certainly his name came to be synonymous with collectors who carried their hobbies to absurd excesses. In the *Tatler*, no. 216, for August 26, 1710, appeared "The Will of a Virtuoso." At his death all Sir Nicholas left to members of his family were such rarities as "a dried cockatrice . . . three crocodile's eggs . . . my last year's collection of grasshoppers . . . my rat's testicles," with "all my flowers, plants, minerals, mosses, shells, pebbles, fossils, beetles, butterflies, caterpillars, grasshoppers and vermin." *Tatler* no. 221 includes a letter from Gimcrack's widow describing his death, which was the result of his pursuing a butterfly across half of England. One of Gimcrack's lineal descendants was "Fossile," the antiquary and collector in Pope and Gay's *Three Hours after Marriage* (1717) in which the Scriblerians had their fun with Dr. John Woodward, one of the great collectors, particularly of fossils.

[22] See Walter E. Houghton, "The English Virtuoso in the Seventeenth Century," *Journal of the History of Ideas*, Nos. 1 and 2 (1942), 51–73, 190–219.

"Virtuoso," as Shadwell used it, involved much more than merely collecting. It is used in the comedy to satirize scientists in general, and in particular those of the Royal Society, who seemed to have followed Bacon in taking all knowledge to be their province. Shadwell's technique anticipates that of Swift in the third book of *Gulliver's Travels,* in which the Grand Academy of Lagado is also a satire upon the experimenters in the Royal Society. For the most part, each writer merely related an actual experiment which sounded absurd to the layman; occasionally Swift combined two real experiments into an absurdity. He picked up more than one detail from Shadwell's *The Virtuoso.*[23]

What of the name, "Gimcrack," Shadwell gave to his virtuoso? Never a familiar term, it might well have passed out of the language had it not been for this comedy. It seems to have been already obsolete in the original sense of "some kind of inlaid wood" and not at all frequent in the two connotations mentioned in the *OED,* both of which Shadwell implied: "a mechanical contrivance" or piece of apparatus, as in its close relative, "knick-knack,"[24] and "an affected person," a show-off. Sir Nicholas had his "knacks," as Shadwell makes clear. In the end he proved to have been only a boasting braggart.

A modern reader or audience is surprised to find that *The Virtuoso* begins with "Bruce in his gown, reading," and reading aloud in Latin. He comments, "Thou great Lucretius! . . . Thou reconcil'st philosophy with verse . . ." (I.i.1–12). The aristocratic audience of Shadwell's time, who could still understand Latin, would have appreciated the introduction of a passage from *De Rerum Natura* and this particular passage, in setting the tone for a scientific comedy. Among the various Gallic enthusiasms brought back to England, when many of the nobles and gentlemen returned from exile with the King, was an interest in the Epicurean philosophy which Gassendi and other philosopher-scientists in France had recently revived. Particularly to the Puritan, Epicureanism and Lucretius were heretical on various counts, specifically on the one implied here: the

---

23 See Nora Mohler and Marjorie Nicolson, "The Scientific Background of Swift's *Voyage to Laputa,*" republished in *Science and Imagination* (Ithaca, 1956), pp. 110–154.

24 *OED* quotes Izaak Walton, *Complete Angler,* Fifth Edition, I, xvi, 263: "Ribbins, and Looking-glasses, and Nut-crackers, and Fiddles, and Hobby horses, and many other gim-cracks, and all the other Finnimbruns that make up a compleat Country Fair."

theory that the universe had emerged through a fortuitous concourse of atoms, not by the power and providence of God, with the corollary that the gods remained aloof with no concern for man. This is the basic theme implied by Bruce in the passage he reads aloud, popularly interpreted in his time as it was to be by Tennyson in the "Song of the Lotos-Eaters":

> . . . to live and lie reclined
> On the hills like Gods together, careless of mankind.

Bruce is a man-about-town, but he is also a young intellectual who in the battle of Ancients and Moderns prided himself on being in the vanguard of modernity. Shadwell's choice of Lucretius was entirely fitting as prelude to a scientific comedy, for Lucretius was the scientific poet *par excellence*.

The scientific interests of Sir Nicholas Gimcrack may be divided broadly into three groups. A few of them look back to the excitement aroused earlier in the century by Galileo's discoveries of the true nature of the universe, reported in the *Sidereus Nuncius* in 1610. Most interesting to lay imagination was his report on the moon, the topography of which indicated that the moon was a smaller world much like our own, with mountains and valleys and—Galileo thought at first—with seas. During the next years astronomers charted moon-maps, pioneers in aerostatics attempted to solve the problems of human flight, and literary imagination ran riot in moon-voyages, serious, fanciful, satiric.[25] Naturally, Sir Nicholas had spent many years compiling a book of geography for the world in the moon (I.ii.242–243). Naturally, also, he was so far advanced in the art of flying that he could already outstrip a bustard (II.ii.30–31). Gimcrack concluded with a sentence that was to echo down the ages: "Nay, I doubt not but in a little time to improve the art so far, 'twill be as common to buy a pair of wings to fly to the world in the moon as to buy a pair of wax boots to ride into Sussex with" (II.ii.33–36). Paraphrased in *The Guardian* of July 20, 1713, it was there attributed to John Wilkins, an attribution which continued until fairly recent times. Shadwell took the passage almost verbatim from Joseph Glanvill.[26]

---

[25] Nicolson, *Voyages to the Moon*, pp. 88–93.

[26] This was first pointed out by F. P. Wilson in an article, "English Letters and the Royal Society," *Mathematical Gazette*, XIV, No. 236 (December, 1935). The passage appeared in Glanvill's *Scepsis Scientifica*,

Such themes as the world in the moon and the possibility of human flight were so familiar as to be almost passé by 1676. Shadwell therefore passes lightly over the discoveries of the telescope and concentrates more heavily on those of the microscope, in which he was up to date almost to the moment. The development of the microscope had been a natural corollary to that of the telescope, though no date can be assigned and no inventor named. Gimcrack's niece Clarinda complains that he "has spent two thousand pounds in microscopes to find out the nature of eels in vinegar, mites in a cheese, and the blue of plums which he has subtly found out to be living creatures" (I.ii.7–10). Whether Gimcrack had made such discoveries or not, Robert Hooke had, and most of the Gimcrack observations can be found in his *Micrographia*, one of the most beautiful books of the Restoration, richly illustrated with pictures of magnified objects.

Popular enthusiasm for the microscope knew no bounds for several years.[27] Bacon had warned his followers that for the advancement of science they must be willing to study "mean and even filthy things." So indeed they did, scientists and laymen alike. There is a whole minor literature of fleas and lice, frogs and toads, rats and mice. Laymen like Samuel Pepys bought themselves microscopes. At first Pepys, like many students in Freshman Biology, could see nothing through his, and, when he saw something, could not identify it until he wisely read Henry Power's *Experimental Philosophy*, the first English book on the subject. A little later glass-grinders found a new buying public among women for whom they manufactured exquisite microscopes which many ladies wore dangling from their bracelets. Just about the time of the composition of *The Virtuoso* reports were reaching the Royal Society of the discoveries of the Dutch Antony van Leeuwenhoek, the first human being to see protozoa and bacteria, a new world of minute life long hidden from the eye. The enthusiasm of Sir Nicholas for the microscope explains the interest he shared with other laymen in lice and other insects (III.iii.1–24) and his

---

London, 1665. Gimcrack's more extensive passage on the moon with the suggestion of warfare with elephants and camels may have been inspired by Samuel Butler's satire on the Royal Society in "The Elephant in the Moon" which was not published until the mid-eighteenth century but seems to have circulated in manuscript among the "Wits."

[27] On the popular interest in the microscope in this period see Marjorie Nicolson, "The Microscope and English Imagination," in *Science and Imagination* (Ithaca, 1956), pp. 155–234.

profound knowledge of ants, spiders, and tarantulas, including the spider Nick whom he had trained as other men trained dogs (III.iii. 69–101). The telescopic-microscopic satire of *The Virtuoso* is part of a large popular pattern which can be paralleled in other Restoration satire as well as more serious literature. More original, because less used by other writers, was Shadwell's satire on a third group of scientific experiments and hypotheses, most of which can be associated with Robert Boyle.

Laughter at the virtuosos, particularly on the part of an aristocratic audience, did not begin with Shadwell. In an entry in his *Diary* for February 1, 1663–1664, Pepys reported a visit to the Duke's Chamber, where the King spent "an hour or two laughing . . . at Gresham College . . . . Gresham College he mightily laughed at, for spending time only in weighing of ayre, and doing nothing else since they sat." His Majesty, who prided himself on his scientific learning and who had his own laboratory, should have understood better than most of the aristocracy the importance of these experiments, which were chiefly those of Robert Boyle with the air-pump.[28] Boyle was familiar with the barometer invented by Torricelli and the Torricellian experiment which first measured atmospheric pressure. He knew the work of Pascal and others in France who proved the Torricellian hypothesis. With Robert Hooke, Boyle had developed an air-pump far superior to that of Otto von Guericke in Germany, with which he laid the basis for many conceptions that lie behind modern science. Boyle was indeed, what Gimcrack aspired to be, "the Universal Philosopher."[29]

Like Boyle, Gimcrack had spent much time in weighing the air; like him, he knew that air is a thinner form of liquid (V.ii.8–9). Boyle had sent agents to different parts of the British Isles and then

[28] An interesting account of Boyle's experiments in this field, intended for the general reader rather than the scientist, will be found in "Robert Boyle's Experiments in Pneumatics," *Harvard Case Histories in Experimental Science*, ed. James Bryant Conant (Cambridge, [Mass.], 1950), No. 1.

[29] See Marie Boas, *Robert Boyle and Seventeenth-Century Chemistry* (Cambridge, 1958), p. 44. "Boyle and his assistants performed a series of brilliant and important experiments, ingenious in conception and far-reaching in their scientific consequences, on the physical properties of air, especially its elasticity, proof of its weight and of the validity of the Torricellian experiment, experiments on dynamics *in vacuo*, on the transmission of light, sound, magnetism, and so on, and experiments on the possibility of combustion and respiration *in vacuo*." Notice Gimcrack's experiments on respiration, II.ii.96–105.

abroad, including the Peak of Teneriffe (IV.iii.256–263), to weigh the air at different altitudes. So Gimcrack had his factors who weighed the air in different parts of Britain and then bottled it up. As other men of quality had their wine cellars, so Gimcrack had his cellar of bottles of air, in which some scenes of the comedy are played. When Gimcrack wanted a change of climate he had no need to travel. Here Gimcrack has gone Boyle one better: Gimcrack's servants merely open bottles of air, and master and guests have all the change they need (IV.iii.240–266).

Experiments of Boyle, too, are the sources of Gimcrack's upon the "lucid sirloin of beef" and the leg of pork by the light of which Sir Nicholas was able to read the Geneva Bible (V.ii.26–32). Although Aristotle left some observations on such matters and may have observed luminescence in fish and flesh, which we now know to result from luminous bacteria, the real study of luminescence remained for modern times. More than one traveler earlier in the seventeenth century had reported seeing "the luminous mutton of Montpelier" in 1640 and 1641. Other observations had been made on shining fish and wood.[30]

Four years before *The Virtuoso* Boyle reported in the *Philosophical Transactions*, December 16, 1672, "Some Observations about Shining Flesh," after his servant had been startled by seeing a brightly luminous leg of veal in the larder. He had been interested in luminescence for several years but at this time he made a series of experiments "to show that the light from luminous flesh, fish and wood is dependent upon the presence of air, and he drew an interesting comparison between the light of shining wood and that of a glowing coal . . . . His 'resemblances' and 'differences' between living light and combustion has become a classic comparison."[31] This time even Gimcrack could not improve on Robert Boyle.

The experiments that must have seemed to some members of the audience the most startling—if they had not followed the Royal

---

[30] A very interesting account of these and a full discussion of scientific work on luminescence may be found in E. Newton Harvey, *A History of Luminescence, from the Earliest Times until 1900*, American Philosophical Society (Philadelphia, 1957). See particularly Chapter IV on the seventeenth century and Chapter XIV, "Shining Fish, Flesh and Wood." Boyle's observations and experiments are discussed in detail, pp. 470–474.

[31] Harvey, p. 470.

Society as faithfully as had Shadwell—were those on blood transfusion (II.ii.109–133). Experiments in transfusion were attempted
in various places, most of them reported to the Royal Society. Pepys
will serve as an excellent guide to the experiments actually performed
by members of the Society, of which he was then a member. On
November 14, 1666, Dr. William Croone told Pepys that at the
meeting of the Society "there was a pretty experiment of the blood
of one dogg let out, till he died, into the body of another on one side,
while all his own run out on the other side. The first died upon the
place, and the other very well, and likely to do well." On November
16, Pepys was told that the recipient dog "is very well, and like to be
so as ever." Naturally the experiment "did give occasion to many
pretty wishes, as of the blood of a Quaker to be let into an Arch-
bishop, and such like." Pepys, like others, however, was persuaded
that in time such experiments would prove "of mighty use to man's
health" (November 14).

Gimcrack's first experiment in transfusion Shadwell picked up not
from this one reported by Pepys but, as Mr. Lloyd has shown and the
vocabulary proves, from one reported to the Society in May of the
same year by Thomas Coxe,[32] who had transfused the blood of a
spaniel into a "mongrel cur with mange." Coxe used the terms
"emittent" and "recipient" as does Gimcrack. Coxe's mangy dog
was cured in ten days; the spaniel seems to have suffered no ill
effects. Gimcrack outdid Coxe in one respect: his "spaniel became a
bulldog and the bulldog a spaniel" (II.ii.127–128).

Gimcrack's later experiment was even more startling since he had
successfully "transfus'd into a human vein sixty-four ounces,
avoirdupois weight, from one sheep" (II.ii.182–184). Again Pepys
will offer evidence. On November 21, 1667, at a tavern, he heard
from John Wilkins and others about an impending experiment to
transfuse sheep's blood into "a man that is a little frantic, that hath
been a kind of minister . . . that is poor and a debauched man, that
the College have hired for 20s. to have some of the blood of a sheep
let into his body; and it is to be done on Saturday next. They purpose
to let in about twelve ounces; which, they compute, is what will be

[32] Coxe's experiment is reported in *Phil. Trans.*, no. 25, May, 1667. Lloyd
also refers to another report immediately preceding this from Edmund
King, who had used a calf and a sheep, the latter of which died. Coxe
transfused 14–16 ounces, King, 49 ounces.

let in in a minute's time by a watch."[33] On Saturday, November 30, 1667, after a meeting of the Royal Society, Pepys noted: "I was pleased to see the person who had his blood taken out. He speaks well, and did this day give the Society a relation thereof in Latin, saying that he finds himself much better since, and as a new man, but he is cracked a little in his head, though he speaks very reasonably, and very well. He had but 20*s*. for his suffering it, and is to have the same again tried upon him: the first sound man that ever had it tried on him in England, and but one that we hear of in France."[34] Sir Nicholas Gimcrack, as usual, improved upon the Royal Society. His madman became ovine not only in temperament but in fact, growing a sheep's tail and sheep's wool, from which Gimcrack planned to have the tailor make his coats.

Of all the scientific satire, the scene (II.ii) that remains most comic is the early one in which Sir Nicholas is "discovered" in his laboratory by Bruce and Longvil, who have made entry into the home of their young ladies by pretending to be ardent young virtuosos. I have reserved it for discussion because it illustrates the basic criticism made by laymen of science, underlying most of the rest. Sir Nicholas is lying on his laboratory table, learning to swim by imitating the motions of a frog in a bowl. His swimming master and his toady stand by

[33] The first English experiment upon a human being, Arthur Coga, is reported in *Phil. Trans.*, no. 30, November 23, 1667. Mr. Lloyd evidently missed this and the French experiments discussed in 34 n., since he considers Gimcrack's transfusion from sheep to man merely exaggeration of the Coxe transfusion. A second transfusion on Arthur Coga was performed on December 12, 1667. No account of this was included in *Phil. Trans.*, but there are numerous contemporary records. For an account of all known seventeenth-century experiments on human transfusion, see Marjorie Nicolson, *Pepys' Diary and the New Science* (University Press of Virginia, forthcoming, 1965).

[34] At least two successful human transfusions had been performed in Paris before the Royal Society experiment on Arthur Coga. See Harcourt Brown, "Jean Denis and the Transfusion of Blood," *Isis*, XXXIX (1948), 15–28. The French experiments were reported in detail to the Royal Society; several accounts appeared in *Phil. Trans.* throughout the year of 1668. Shadwell seems to have followed these with some care, since his allusion to gangrene (II.ii.216–218) would seem to have been to a Swedish baron who died after (though not as a result of) transfusion, who proved to be suffering from gangrene. Shadwell's maniac was less Coga, who was only a little "touched," than a raving maniac on whom Jean Denis performed two transfusions in Paris. The lurid story can be found in Harcourt Brown's article.

admiringly. In answer to Longvil's inquiry whether he has tried to swim in water, Gimcrack replies, "Never, sir. I hate the water." What, then, asks Longvil, is the use of swimming? "I content myself," says Gimcrack, "with the speculative part of swimming; I care not for the practic. I seldom bring anything to use; 'tis not my way. Knowledge is my ultimate end." The layman, then as now, was capable of understanding what Bacon called Experiments of Fruit—applied science or technology—but, like the aristocrats in the Duke's Chamber, he often was dumb and blind before Experiments of Light—pure science—which must precede the fruit.

So far as Sir Nicholas, the virtuoso, is concerned, the denouement begins when his house is surrounded by a group of weavers enraged because they have heard that Gimcrack has invented an automatic loom that will put them out of work. Actually the theme was suggested earlier in connection with the stentrophonical tube Gimcrack planned to develop, by means of which a human voice might be heard throughout a county. When it has been perfected, the King will find it a service, since "there needs but one parson to preach to a whole county. The king may then take all the church lands into his own hands." But what of the parsons? inquires Longvil, to which Gimcrack replies in effect, "Let 'em eat cake" (V.ii.43–68). A modern reader may be surprised to find that the distrust of "labor" for automation goes back so far. Actually, it had begun well before the seventeenth century, probably always coexistent with the advance of technology.[35]

The Royal Society was fully aware of the opposition the advancement of science would face from the working classes. Indeed, Thomas Sprat devoted a long section of his *History* to this theme, "to stop the undeserv'd clamors which perhaps in this humorous Age some Tradesmen may raise against the Royal Society . . . . That the growth of new Inventions and new Artifices will infallibly reduce all the old

[35] Among reflections of this theme in popular literature, I was interested to find at the Huntington Library: [Thomas Powell], *Humane Industry: or A History of the Manual Arts, Deducing the Original, Progress, and Improvement of them* (London, 1661). He tells the following story: "In Dantzick in Poland there was set up a rare invention for weaving of 4 or five Webs at a time without any humane help; it was an Automaton or Engine that moved of it self and would work night and day; which invention was supprest, because it would prejudice the poor people of the Town; and the Artificer was made away secretly (as 'tis conceived) as Lancellotti the Italian Abbot relates out of the mouth of Mr. Muller a Polonian that had seen the device."

ones to poverty and decay."[36] On the contrary, Sprat insisted, the advancement of science will open many more doors than it will close, affording men opportunities far in excess of those they have at present. In concluding, he drew the attention of the English to the fact that Holland threatened to outstrip England for the very reason that the Dutch, unlike the English, had not been "averse to new inventions" but were seizing every opportunity for the advancement both of science and of technology. The weavers who threaten Gimcrack's property and life are clearly trueborn Englishmen. Finally the great Virtuoso makes a complete and ignominious confession. Never in all his life has he invented anything, "not even an engine with which to pare cream cheese."

MARJORIE HOPE NICOLSON

The Institute for Advanced Study, Princeton

DAVID STUART RODES

Stanford University

In preparing this edition Professor Nicolson wrote the commentary on Shadwell's satire on the new science and most of the explanatory notes; Mr. Rodes wrote the bibliographical account of the text and prepared the text.

---

[36] *History of the Royal Society of London* (London, 1667), Section XXIV, pp. 378 ff.

THE VIRTUOSO

TO THE MOST ILLUSTRIOUS PRINCE, WILLIAM, DUKE OF NEWCASTLE, ETC.

May it please your Grace,

So long as your Grace persists in obliging, I must go on in acknowledging; nor can I let any opportunity pass of telling 5 the world how much I am favored by you; or any occasion slip of assuring your Grace that all the actions of my life shall be dedicated to your service, who, by your noble patronage, your generosity and kindness, and your continual bounty, have made me wholly your creature; nor can I forbear to 10 declare that I am more obliged to your Grace than to all mankind. And my misfortune is, I can make no other return but a declaration of my grateful resentments.

When I show'd your Grace some part of this comedy at Welbeck, being all that I had then written of it, you were 15 pleased to express your great liking of it which was a sufficient encouragement for me to proceed in it, and when I had finish'd it, to lay it humbly at your feet. Whatever I write, I will submit to your Grace, who are the greatest master of wit, the most exact observer of mankind, and the most 20 accurate judge of humor that ever I knew. And were I not assured of the greatness of your favor, I should be afraid of the excellency of your judgment.

I have endeavored in this play at humor, wit, and satire, which are the three things, however I may have 25 fallen short in my attempt, which your Grace has often told me are the life of a comedy. Four of the humors are entirely new, and, without vanity, I may say I ne'er produc'd a comedy that had not some natural humor in it not

---

2. *William, Duke of Newcastle*] In addition to his career in the state and in the Royalist forces, William Cavendish, Duke of Newcastle (1592–1676), was a dramatist and a well-known patron of the arts. Ben Jonson had written for him, and he had supported Shirley and Davenant, and later Dryden, Shadwell, and Flecknoe. Langbaine wrote of him: "Since the time of Augustus, no person better understood or more generously encouraged poets; so that we may truly call him our English Macaenas." His dramas were the following: *The Country Captain*, *The Variety*, *The Triumphant Widow*, and *The Humorous Lovers*.

13. *resentments*] grateful appreciation or acknowledgment.

represented before, nor I hope never shall. Nor do I count   30
those humors which a great many do, that is to say, such as
consist in using one or two bywords, or in having a fantastic,
extravagant dress, as many pretended humors have, nor in
the affectation of some French words which several plays
have shown us. I say nothing of impossible, unnatural farce   35
fools, which some intend for comical who think it the
easiest thing in the world to write a comedy and yet will
sooner grow rich upon their ill plays than write a good one.
Nor is downright silly folly a humor, as some take it to be,
for 'tis a mere natural imperfection; and they might as well   40
call it a humor of blindness in a blind man, or lameness in a
lame one. Or as a celebrated French farce has the humor of
one who speaks very fast and of another who speaks very
slow, but natural imperfections are not fit subjects for
comedy since they are not to be laugh'd at but pitied. But   45
the artificial folly of those who are not coxcombs by nature
but with great art and industry make themselves so is a
proper object of comedy, as I have discoursed at large in
the preface to *The Humorists*, written five years since. Those
slight, circumstantial things mentioned before are not   50
enough to make a good comical humor which ought to be
such an affectation as misguides men in knowledge, art, or
science, or that causes defection in manners and morality, or
perverts their minds in the main actions of their lives. And
this kind of humor I think I have not improperly described   55
in the epilogue to *The Humorists*.

But your Grace understands humor too well not to know
this and much more than I can say of it. All I have now to
do is humbly to dedicate this play to your Grace, which
has succeeded beyond my expectation, and the humors of   60
which have been approved by men of the best sense and
learning. Nor do I hear of any professed enemies to the play
but some women, and some men of feminine understandings,
who like slight plays only that represent a little tattle sort of
conversation like their own; but true humor is not liked or   65

30. never] *Q1*; ever *Q2-3*.   58. than] *Q2-3;* then *Q1*.

---

42. *French farce*] Molière's *L'Amour Médicin*, produced at Versailles in
1665.

understood by them, and therefore even my attempt towards it is condemned by them. But the same people, to my great comfort, damn all Mr. Jonson's plays, who was incomparably the best dramatic poet that ever was, or, I believe, ever will be; and I had rather be author of one scene in his   70
best comedies than of any play this age has produced. That there are a great many faults in the conduct of this play, I am not ignorant. But I, having no pension but from the theater, which is either unwilling or unable to reward a man sufficiently for so much pains as correct comedies require,   75
cannot allot my whole time to the writing of plays, but am forced to mind some other business of advantage. Had I as much money and as much time for it, I might perhaps write as correct a comedy as any of my contemporaries. But I hope your Grace will accept of this with all its imperfections,   80
which, since the Royal Family have received favorably, I have all my aim if it be approved by your Grace who are, next to them, in the greatest esteem and observance of

My Lord,

London, June   Your Grace's
26, 1676.   Most obliged, humble servant,
                 THOMAS SHADWELL

68. Jonson's]   Johnson's   *Q 1–3*
throughout.

PROLOGUE

You come with such an eager appetite
To a late play which gave so great delight,
Our poet fears that by so rich a treat
Your palates are become too delicate.
Yet since you've had rhyme for a relishing bit   5
To give a better taste to comic wit.
But this requires expense of time and pains
Too great, alas, for poets' slender gains.
For wit, like china, should long buried lie
Before it ripens to good comedy: 10
A thing we ne'er have seen since Jonson's days,
And but a few of his were perfect plays.
Now drudges of the stage must oft appear;
They must be bound to scribble twice a year.
Thus the thin, threadbare vicar still must toil,   15
While the fat, lazy doctor bears the spoil.
In the last comedy some wits were shown;
In this are fools that much infest the town.
Plenty of fops, grievances of the age,
Whose nauseous figures ne'er were on a stage.   20
He cannot say they'll please you, but they're new;
And he hopes you will say, he has drawn 'em true.
He's sure in wit he can't excel the rest;
He'd but be thought to write a fool the best.
Such fools as haunt and trouble men of wit,   25
And spite of them will for their pictures sit.
Yet no one coxcomb in this play is shown;
No one man's humor makes a part alone,
But scatter'd follies gather'd into one.
He says, if with new fops he can but please,   30
He'll twice a year produce as new as these.

22. he has] *Q1–2;* h' has *Q3.*

−7−

Dramatis Personae

Sir Nicholas Gimcrack, *the Virtuoso*
Sir Formal Trifle, *the Orator, a florid coxcomb*
Snarl, *an old, pettish fellow, a great admirer of the last age and a*
    declaimer against the vices of this, and privately very vicious himself
Sir Samuel Hearty, *a brisk, amorous, adventurous, unfortunate*   5
    coxcomb; one that by the help of humorous, nonsensical bywords takes
    himself to be a wit
Longvil, *in love with Miranda*⎫
Bruce, *in love with Clarinda* ⎬ *Gentlemen of wit and sense*
Swimming Master   ⎭   10
Hazard, [*Lady Gimcrack's lover*]

Lady Gimcrack, *wife to the Virtuoso*
Clarinda, *in love with Longvil*⎫
Miranda, *in love with Bruce*   ⎬ *Nieces to the Virtuoso*   15
[Mrs.] Flirt, *the Virtuoso's whore*
[Mrs.] Figgup, *Snarl's whore*
Betty, *Clarinda's chambermaid*
Bridget, *Lady Gimcrack's maid*   20
Porter *to Sir Nicholas*
     Ribbon Weavers, Sick and Lame People, Porters,
     Servants, [Steward *to Sir Nicholas*], Masqueraders

Scene: *London*

7. a wit] *Q 1–2;* a great wit *Q 3.*

The Virtuoso

ACT I

[I.i]   Bruce *in his gown, reading.*

BRUCE.

Thou great Lucretius! Thou profound oracle of wit and
sense! Thou art no trifling, landskip poet, no fantastic,
heroic dreamer with empty descriptions of impossibilities
and mighty-sounding nothings. Thou reconcil'st philosophy
with verse and dost almost alone demonstrate that poetry   5
and good sense may go together. (*Reads.*)

> omnis enim per se divum natura necessest
> immortali aevo summa cum pace fruatur
> semota ab nostris rebus seiunctaque longe.
> nam'privata dolore omni, privata periclis,   10
> ipsa suis pollens opibus, nil indiga nostri,
> nec bene promeritis capitur neque tangitur ira.

Enter Longvil.

7. *necessest*] *Bailey ed.,* (*see expl.*)   9. *ab*] *Bailey ed.; a* Q 1–3.
note, ll. 7–12, below); *necesse est*   11. *nil*] *Bailey ed.; nihil* Q 1–3.
Q 1–3.

7–12. *omnis . . . ira.*] text as edited by Cyrillus Bailey, [Titi] Lucreti
[Cari], *De Rerum Natura*, Editio Altera (Oxonii, n.d.), II, 646–651.

> The Gods, by right of Nature, must possess
> An everlasting Age of perfect Peace:
> Far off removed from us and our Affairs;
> Neither approached by Dangers, or by Cares;
> Rich in themselves, to whom we cannot add:
> Not pleased by Good Deeds; nor provoked by Bad.

Translated by John Wilmot, Earl of Rochester, about 1676. The lines
appear as No. 40 in his complete poems, *Poems by John Wilmot, Earl of
Rochester*, Muses Library, sec. ed. 1964, ed. Vivian de Sola Pinto, pp. 49–50.
For recent studies of Lucretius in this period, see Wolfgang Bernard
Fleischmann, *Lucretius and English Literature* (Paris, 1963); Mary Gallagher,
"Dryden's Translation of Lucretius," *Huntington Library Quarterly*, XXVIII
(1964), 19–30.

LONGVIL.

> Bruce, good morrow. What great author art thou chewing the cud upon? I look'd to have found you with your headache and your morning qualms. 15

BRUCE.

> We should not live always hot-headed; we should give ourselves leave sometimes to think.

LONGVIL.

> Lucretius! Divine Lucretius! But my noble Epicurean, what an unfashionable fellow art thou, that in this age art given to understand Latin. 20

BRUCE.

> 'Tis true, Longvil. I am a bold fellow to pretend to it when 'tis accounted pedantry for a gentleman to spell and where the race of gentlemen is more degenerated than that of horses.

LONGVIL.

> It must needs be so, for gentlemen care not upon what 25 strain they get their sons, nor how they breed 'em when they have got 'em. The best of 'em now have a kind of education like pages, and you shall seldom see a young fellow of this age that does not look like one of those overgrown animals newly manumitted from trunk breeches. 30

BRUCE.

> Some are first instructed by ignorant, young, household pedants, who dare not whip the dunces, their pupils, for fear of their lady mothers. Then before they can construe and parse they are sent into France with sordid, illiterate creatures call'd dried-nurses or governors, engines of as 35 little use as pacing-saddles and as unfit to govern 'em as the post-horses they ride to Paris on. From whence they return with a little smattering of that mighty "Universal language" without being ever able to write true English.

LONGVIL.

> O but then they'll value 'em for speaking good French. 40

BRUCE.

> Perhaps good French may be spoken with little sense, but good English cannot.

---

38. "*Universal language*"] French was gradually replacing Latin as the international language of diplomacy.

LONGVIL.

Thou art in the right. But then there are a sort of hopeful
youths that do not travel; and they are either such as keep
company with their sisters and visit their kindred and are a   45
great comfort to their mothers and a scorn to all others, or
they are sparks that early break loose from discipline and at
sixteen, forsooth, set up for men of the town.

BRUCE.

Such as come drunk and screaming into a playhouse and
stand upon the benches and toss their full periwigs and   50
empty heads and with their shrill unbroken pipes cry,
"Damn me, this is a damn'd play. Prithee, let's to a whore,
Jack." Then says another with great gallantry pulling out
his box of pills, "Damn me, Tom, I am not in a condition.
Here's my turpentine for my third clap," when you   55
would think he was not old enough to be able to get
one.

LONGVIL.

Heav'n be prais'd, these youths, like untimely fruit, are
like to be rotten before they are ripe!

BRUCE.

These are sure the only animals that live without think-   60
ing. A sensible plant has more imagination than most of
'em.

LONGVIL.

Gad, if they go on as they begin, the gentlemen of the next
age will scarce have learning enough to claim the benefit
of the clergy for manslaughter.   65

BRUCE.

The highest pitch our youth do generally arrive at is to have a
form, a fashion of wit, a routine of speaking, which they
get by imitation; and generally they imitate the extrava-
gancies of witty men drunk, which they very discreetly
practice sober, but in so clumsy and awkward a way that   70
methinks it should make witty men out of love with their
vices, as prentices wearing pantaloons would make gentlemen lay by the habit.

LONGVIL.

These are sad truths, but I am not such a fop to disquiet
myself one minute for a thousand of 'em.   75

BRUCE.

You have reason; say what we can, the beastly, restive
world will its own way, and there is not so foolish a creature
as a reformer.

LONGVIL.

Thank Heav'n I am not such a public spirited fop to lose
one moment of my private pleasure for all that can happen   80
without me.

BRUCE.

Thou art a philosopher; and now thou talk'st of private
pleasure, what think'st thou of our adventure with Clarinda
and Miranda, the Virtuoso's, Sir Nicholas Gimcrack's,
nieces? See the danger of going to church, Longvil. I   85
advised thee against it; 'twas a fine curiosity and has cost
us dear.

LONGVIL.

Did ever I think we two should be caught any way in a
church?

BRUCE.

'Tis a little strange that we that have run together into   90
all the vices of men of wit and gentlemen should at last
together fall into the vice of fools and country squires: love.

LONGVIL.

We that have wonder'd at all other amorous coxcombs must
now laugh at one another. I am amaz'd at thy passion for
Clarinda.   95

BRUCE.

And I no less at thine for Miranda. There's witchcraft in't,
to love where there's such apparent difficulty, for Virtuoso
is as jealous as an Italian uncle. His jealousy, helped by the
vigilancy and malice of that impertinent strumpet his wife,
keeps 'em from all manner of address. Letters they have   100
receiv'd from us, and we can have no answer. What the
devil's left for us to do in this case?

LONGVIL.

Fall down and worship me! I have found out the noblest

77. own] *Q1; om. Q2–3.*

---

76. *You have reason*] The French construction from *vous avez raison* is
ironic in light of lines 31–42 above.

tool to work with and the most excellent coxcomb that
nature e'er began or art e'er finish'd.   105

BRUCE.

Thou reviv'st my dying hope. Who is't?

LONGVIL.

A rascal that is Virtuoso's admirer, flatterer, and great
confidant, the only man he'll trust his nieces with, who has
discover'd to me that he has a passion for your Clarinda.

BRUCE.

Curse on him. But a rival's a very improper instrument.   110

LONGVIL.

But this is a rival so conceited of his own parts that he can
never be jealous of another's. He is indeed a very choice
spirit, the greatest master of tropes and figures, the most
Ciceronian coxcomb, the noblest orator breathing. He never
speaks without flowers of rhetoric. In short, he is very much 115
abounding in words and very much defective in sense:
Sir Formal Trifle.

BRUCE.

He's an original indeed, the most florid knight alive. I have
some little knowledge of him.

LONGVIL.

I have persuaded him that you and I are the greatest 120
philosophers and the greatest admirers of the Virtuoso and
his works that can be. This has already produc'd that good
effect that Sir Formal has this morning been with me from
his noble friend Sir Nicholas to invite me to come to his
house to see a cock-lobster dissected and afterwards to dine 125
with him, and will be here with the same message to you.

BRUCE.

How I applaud thy wit! But why wouldst not thou communicate thy design beforehand?

LONGVIL.

I was resolv'd to surprise thee with it if it took and to
conceal it if it did not.   130

Enter Bruce's Footman.

FOOTMAN.

Sir, Sir Samuel Hearty has sent you word he will come and
give you a visit.   [*Exit.*]

BRUCE.

There's an ass, an original of another kind; one that
thinks that all mirth consists in noise, tumult, and violent
laughter; at once the merriest and the dullest rogue alive; 135
one that affects a great many nonsensical bywords which
he takes to be wit and uses upon all occasions.

LONGVIL.

But the best part of his character is behind: he is the most
amorous coxcomb; the most designing and adventurous
knight alive; a great masquerader, and has forty several 140
disguises to make love in; and has been the most unlucky
fellow breathing in that and all other adventures. He has
never made love where he was not refus'd, nor wag'd war
where he was not beaten. Here he is.

Enter Sir Samuel.

SIR SAMUEL.

Tom Bruce, good morrow to thee. Dear Jack Longvil, how 145
dost do? 'Faith I wish'd you with me last night. We were a
knot of merry rogues of thirteen or fourteen of us got
together, sung, and tore, and roar'd, and ranted egad all
weathers, and drunk, and laugh'd dagger out o'sheath, I
vow to Gad. We were upon the high ropes, i'faith. Hey 150
poop, troll—Come aloft boys—Ha-ha-ha. Ah rogues, that
you had been with us, i'faith. Ha-ha-ha.

BRUCE.

'Faith and would we had.

SIR SAMUEL.

Egad boys, we'd have paid you off. We swing'd it away,
i'faith. We were so merry, o'my conscience, you might have 155
heard us half a mile.

LONGVIL.

What a divine hearing was that!

SIR SAMUEL.

'Faith I was pure company; I was never on a better pin
in my life. There was one of the company would needs
pretend to be a wit, forsooth; but i'faith boys, I run him 160
down so, the devil take me, he had not a word to throw at a
dog about business. Whenever he was impertinent, I took
him up with my old repartee: Peace, said I, *Tace* is Latin

for a candle; and whene'er he began again, *Tace* is Latin
for a candle again said I. Thus I run him down with a hey 165
poop! whoo! ha-ha-ha! He had not a word, not one word,
I vow to Gad. Ha-ha-ha.

LONGVIL (*to* Bruce).

As this fellow thinks all mirth consists in noise, so he thinks
all wit is in running a man down, as he calls it, not considering that impudence does that better.   170

SIR SAMUEL.

'Faith I was very frolic, and there came a fellow abruptly
into our company. I whipp'd up to him, hey, slapdash, gave
him a kick in the arse to drink, and made pilgarlic go ten
times faster downstairs than he came up, i'faith boys.

BRUCE.

But this may cost you a challenge, Sir Samuel.   175

SIR SAMUEL.

Challenge! Egad if he does challenge me, I'll run him
through the lungs about that business. He shall not only
blow out a candle with his wound, but the sun shall shine
through him. Pox, he's a raw fellow; he does not know
what 'tis to have a towel drawn through his body.   180

LONGVIL [*to* Bruce].

This fellow's brains, like some bottle-beer, fly all into froth.

BRUCE [*to* Longvil].

So brisk and dull a rogue I never saw.

SIR SAMUEL.

Come, 'faith we are choice lads and should make much of
one another. I have indeed tonight an *intriguo* with a lady; I
am to venture in a disguise. I give a masquerade; you know 185
and, I hope, will be there. But tomorrow night, 'faith I'll be
very drunk about business. Ha boys, ha-ha.

Enter Bruce's Footman.

172. up to him] *Q1;* him up to   184–185. I am] *Q1;* and I am
Q2; him up too *Q3.*   *Q2–3.*

164–165. *Tace . . . candle*] *Tace* is a Latin imperative "be silent." The
phrase is intended to be a humorously veiled hint to someone to be still,
implying particularly that the user is an educated man speaking to illiterates.

173. *pilgarlic*] bald head, with indecent connotations; an appellation
first given to "pilled" or bald head, ludicrously likened to the peeled head
of garlic, and then to a bald-headed man; sometimes with insinuations as
to an alleged cause.

FOOTMAN.

>Sir, one Sir Formal Trifle bids me tell you he's come to pay
>his *devoir* to you. He charg'd me to use that expression; I
>know not what he means by it. 190

BRUCE.

>'Twas very quaintly expressed. Desire him to come up.

>[*Exit* Footman.]

SIR SAMUEL.

>O I have often seen him at Sir Nicholas Gimcrack's house,
>the Virtuoso. 'Faith of a grave fellow, he's a very in-
>genious rogue, and egad he has a fine way with him.

LONGVIL.

>I never knew any man that had a way with him (as they call 195
>it) that was not a coxcomb.

SIR SAMUEL.

>He has a notable vein of oratory, a brave delivery; and
>when he is in the humor, egad he'll speak finely, finely, very
>finely.

Enter Sir Formal Trifle.

SIR FORMAL.

>Gentlemen, I humbly kiss all your hands in general, but 200
>(*to* Bruce)   sir, yours in a more particular manner.

BRUCE.

>Sir Formal, your most humble servant. You do me a great
>deal of honor in this visit.

SIR FORMAL.

>Sir, I never could admit a thought within the slender
>sphere of my imagination that could once suggest to me 205
>the not meeting with a good reception from a person that is
>so strictly oblig'd by and so nicely practic'd in the severer
>rules and stricter methods of honor as you are.

BRUCE.

>Sir, you oblige me with your fair character.

SIR FORMAL.

>Upon my sincerity, I wholly eschew all oratory and 210
>compliments with persons of your worth and generosity.
>And though I must confess upon due occasions I am
>extremely delighted with those pretty, spruce expressions
>wherewith wit and eloquence use to trick up human

thoughts, and with the gaudy dress that smoother pens so 215
finely clothe them in, yet I never us'd the least tincture of
rhetoric with my friend, which I hope you'll do me the
honor to let me call you. (*Aside.*) I think I am florid.

SIR SAMUEL [*to* Longvil].
I told you i'faith he'd speak notably. He has a silver
tongue.   220

LONGVIL [*to* Sir Samuel].
O yes, a golden one. [*Aside.*] What would such coxcombs
do if there were not greater to admire them? This Sir Formal
is call'd a well-spoken man, with a pox to him.

BRUCE.
Sir, I shall think myself honored with the title of your
servant.   225

SIR FORMAL.
It is so much to my advantage that I do assure you Sir
Formal Trifle shall never give Mr. Bruce any occasion to
believe that he will omit any opportunity of avowing himself to all the world to be the most humble and obedient
of his servants. —Sweet Mr. Longvil, having already this 230
morning paid my *devoir* to you, I shall at present only tell
you that which I hope is no news to you: to wit, that I am
your most humble servant. [*Aside.*] There, I think I
was concise and florid.

LONGVIL.
You do me too much honor.   235

BRUCE [*to* Longvil].
Is there so great a rascal upon earth as an orator, that
would slur and top upon our understandings and impose his
false conceits for true reasoning and his florid words for
good sense?

LONGVIL [*to* Bruce].
Your bully with his false dice and box is an honester man. 240

SIR FORMAL (*to* Sir Samuel).
Truly sir, I am afflicted at the late falling out between
Sir Nicholas and your noble self, which has deprived me of
so frequently enjoying the honor of kissing your fair hands
there.

228. will] *Q1;* shall *Q2–3.*   233. S.D.] *Q3; om. Q1–2.*

SIR SAMUEL.

O Lord, sir, your servant, your servant, 'faith I am very 245
sorry for't too. But I shall be glad to wait upon you and
drink his health in a glass of Burgundy and be very merry
about business. He's a fine person 'faith, though he does not
care much for wit.

SIR FORMAL.

And now, Mr. Bruce, after these little digressions which my 250
particular esteem of every person in this presence has
engag'd me to, I am to inform you that my noble friend
Sir Nicholas Gimcrack does by me invite you with your
friend, being philosophers and consequently his admirers,
to come to his house this forenoon to see the dissection of a 255
little animal commonly called a Chichester cock-lobster and
afterwards to take a dish of meat and discourse of the noble
operation and to sport an author over a glass of wine.

SIR SAMUEL [aside].

Ha! This will prove for my design.

LONGVIL [aside].

Give me your orator for dispatch. What a flourish the rogue 260
has made to invite us to dinner.

BRUCE.

Sir, I will not do myself the injure to fail two such ingenious and learned men as Sir Nicholas and yourself.

SIR FORMAL.

Alas, sir, I! I am but his shadow, his humble admirer,
but I will undertake for him. Fame has not promis'd more 265
of him to your expectation than he will perform to your
understanding. Trust me, he is the finest speculative gentleman in the whole world and in his cogitations the most
serene animal alive. Not a creature so little but affords him
great curiosities. He is the most admirable person in the 270
meletetiques, viz., in reflections and meditations, in the
whole world. Not a creature so inanimate to which he does
not give a tongue, he makes the whole world vocal; he makes
flowers, nay, weeds, speak eloquently and by a noble kind of

246. for't] *Q1;* fort't *Q2;* for it *Q3.*   262. injure] *Q1–2;* injury *Q3.*

---

258. *to . . . author*] to discuss an author.
271. *meletetiques*] obs. Greek neuter plural; rules or methods of meditation.

prosopopeia instruct mankind. And, sir, though I ignore not 275
what the envy of detractors have express'd of him, yet, in
short, I opine him to be the most curious and inquisitive
philosopher breathing; and I will let him know you intend
to wait on him. Within two hours he will show. 'Tis his time
of operation.   280

BRUCE.

We will not fail. [*To* Longvil.]   What an employment
has this fool under him! He is the chorus to his puppet show.

LONGVIL [*to* Bruce].

I would rather be trumpeter to a monster and call in the
rabble to see a calf with six legs than show such a blockhead.

SIR SAMUEL.

Pray sir, commend me heartily to Sir Nicholas, and tell him 285
faith and troth I am sorry my wit should offend him, and I
shall henceforth endeavor to be as dull as I can to merit his
esteem. I confess I was a little too airy and brisk about that
business, but 'faith I am his most humble servant and have
a sword and arm at his service, and 'gad will draw it against 290
any man breathing in defence of his person and philosophy.
And so let him know from Sir Samuel.

SIR FORMAL.

I shall perform your commands, and doubt not but to do
you service in it. Gentlemen, again I kiss your hands.   *Exit.*

LONGVIL.

Sir Samuel, how came your wit to offend the Virtuoso?   295

SIR SAMUEL.

'Faith I was very well there, but you know I am an airy,
brisk, merry fellow, and facetious, and his grave philosophical humor did not agree with mine. Besides, he does not
value wit at all; he won't be pleas'd with you, I assure you.

BRUCE.

Why so?   300

SIR SAMUEL.

Why, he did not like me at all; he's an enemy to wit as all
virtuosos are.

BRUCE.

Sure if he had lik'd wit, he would have lik'd you.

---

275. *prosopopeia*] a rhetorical figure by which an abstract or inanimate
thing is represented as a person; personification.

SIR SAMUEL.

> That I think without vanity. But you must know, I pretended to Miranda.   305

LONGVIL [*aside*].

> Pox on him, what says he?

SIR SAMUEL.

> And, not to boast, I found my love would have had a good reception, but her malicious sister, Clarinda, discover'd my *intriguo*, and Sir Nicholas forbade me his house upon that business.   310

BRUCE.

> What exception had he against you?

SIR SAMUEL.

> Why faith he would not dispose of his niece to a wit, he said.

LONGVIL.

> A wit! 'Faith he might as well have call'd thee a dromedary.

SIR SAMUEL.

> Peace, I say; *Tace* is Latin for a candle. Ha-ha-ha. You 315 know I can run you down. In short, he said I was a wit, a flashy wit. But if you have any kindness in the world for me, you might help me in this *intriguo*.

BRUCE.

> How so?

SIR SAMUEL.

> Now you are invited, let me wait on you in a livery for one of 320 your footmen. I have forty several periwigs for these *intriguos* and businesses. 'Gad if you will, whip slapdash, I'll bring this business about as round as a hoop.

> [Bruce *and* Longvil *talk apart.*]

BRUCE.

> Prithee, Longvil, let him go that we may make sport with him and abuse the rogue damnably.   325

LONGVIL.

> 'Sdeath! What, bring him to my mistress!

BRUCE.

> Canst thou be jealous of so silly a rascal?

LONGVIL.

> 'Tis ill trusting the fantastic appetites of women. They are subject to the greensickness of the mind as well as that

of the body: one makes them love fools and blockheads as 330
the other does dirt and charcoal.

BRUCE.

She's a woman of wit. Besides, let him wear your livery,
and by your prerogative you may kick your rival all this day
if he should be fancy, which he will certainly be.

LONGVIL.

That consideration prevails with me.   335

SIR SAMUEL.

What say you, boys? Is it not an admirable *intriguo*? Ha!

LONGVIL.

Sir Samuel, there is some difficulty, but to serve you we can
refuse nothing. You shall do me the honor to wear a livery of
mine. I have new ones come home this morning. My man
will give you one.   340

SIR SAMUEL.

If I do not do my business, Jack, I am the son of a tinderbox.

LONGVIL.

Well, pray Mr. Tinderbox, go about it quickly.

SIR SAMUEL.

Gad I'll do't instantly, in the twinkling of a bedstaff.
Ha-ha-ha.

BRUCE.

In the twinkling of what?   345

SIR SAMUEL.

Hey, pull away rogues, in the twinkling of a bedstaff—a
witty way I have of expressing myself. I'll away.   *Exit.*

LONGVIL.

Was there ever so senseless a fop? Words are no more to him
than breaking wind: they only give him vent. They serve
not with him to express thoughts, for he does not think.   350

BRUCE.

A wit! A flashy wit! A flashy wit! What a dull villain is this
virtuoso. But prithee take all occasions to kick this flashy
wit much; he'll give thee enough.

LONGVIL.

Pox on him, he has read Seneca. He cares not for kicking.
He never scap'd kicking in any disguise he ever put on.   355

341. do not do] *Q1;* do not *Q2–3.*

-21-

BRUCE.

Nor in any of his own habits neither. But I'll in and dress
me.   *Exeunt.*

[I.ii]   *Enter* Miranda *and* Clarinda *in the garden.*

MIRANDA.

Were ever women so confin'd in England by a foolish
uncle worse than an Italian? But that I should be loath to
speak ill of the dead, I should think my father was not
compos mentis when he made his will to bequeath us to the
government of a virtuoso only because his first wife was our   5
aunt.

CLARINDA.

A sot that has spent two thousand pounds in microscopes to
find out the nature of eels in vinegar, mites in a cheese, and
the blue of plums which he has subtly found out to be
living creatures.   10

MIRANDA.

One who has broken his brains about the nature of maggots,
who has studied these twenty years to find out the several
sorts of spiders, and never cares for understanding mankind.

CLARINDA.

Shall we never get free from his jealousy and the malice of
his impertinent wife?   15

MIRANDA.

Though he be jealous of us, yet he's as tame a civil London
husband to his wife as she can wish, who certainly cuckolds
him abundantly.

CLARINDA.

She hates us in her heart because she thinks we see too
much. To be confin'd, and to such impertinence too, puts   20
me beyond all patience.

MIRANDA.

'Twill make dogs curst to be tied up, and sure 'twill provoke
free-born women more.

0.1.] *scene division om. Q 1–3.*

---

4. *compos mentis*] sane in mind.
22. *curst*] savage, vicious.

CLARINDA.

We should have as good company in a jail, for none but
quacks and fools come hither, and one of the worst of 'em is   25
my foolish, florid coxcomb, Sir Formal.

MIRANDA.

He has banish'd my coxcomb, Sir Samuel, a brisk, airy fool
that there is some diversion in. He had as many tricks as a
well-educated spaniel, would fetch, and carry, and come
over a stick for the king. He had some tricks of a man too,   30
and may pass muster among the young, gay fellows of this
town, and could sing all the new tunes and songs at the
playhouses.

CLARINDA.

And we are troubled with an old fellow here in the house, his
uncle Snarl, a great declaimer against the vices of the age,   35
a clownish, blunt, satirical fellow, a hater of all young
people and new fashions.

MIRANDA.

But he is such a froward, testy old fellow he should be
wormed like a mad dog.

CLARINDA.

We try his patience sometimes, but I am pleas'd to hear   40
him abuse the Virtuoso his nephew, who bears all in hope of
his estate. Snarl is a fellow spares nobody, always speaks
what he thinks, and does what he pleases. But yet, Miranda,
there's a worse misfortune than all this: that we two should,
in a church when we should ha' been thinking of something   45
else, fall in love with two men of wit and pleasure who are
too much men of the town to think of marriage, we being
too little women of the town to think of any other love.

MIRANDA.

We have fortunes good enough to lure them to matrimony
if that were all, but the worst part of the story is, he whom   50
I love is in love with you, and your man makes addresses
to me as their letters tell us. And even these men we cannot
see but at church or at a playhouse when we are guarded
by our malicious, watchful aunt.

48. too] *Q 1, 3;* two *Q 2.*
51. you] *Q 1, 3;* yon *Q 2.*

CLARINDA.

    If we could but see these men privately, there yet might be   55
some hopes. We might each of us use our lover scurvily, and
him we love we might charm with kindness, for they are men
that have known the pomps and vanities of this wicked world
too much to love a face only.

MIRANDA.

    If we could bring this about, I would stand out at nothing   60
that might procure our freedom. The mischief is, if we rebel
Virtuoso will allow us nothing out of our fortunes till we
come of age.

CLARINDA.

    Then we must e'en live upon the credit of a reversion as
some young fellows do that with their fathers hang'd. I   65
warrant thee we'll find credit.

MIRANDA.

    And lose our reputations. We have much ado to keep 'em as
we are.

CLARINDA.

    Let what will come on't, I am resolved to break out. He
shall sooner stop a tide than my inclinations.   70

MIRANDA.

    O, if your knight-errants and we agree upon the point,
they'll soon deliver us distressed damsels from our
enchanted castle.

Enter Snarl *and his man.*

SNARL [*to his man*].

    'Tis a fine morning. Fetch me a pipe of tobacco and a
match into the garden.   *Exit Man.*   75

CLARINDA [*to* Miranda].

    Here's old Snarl. He has call'd for his tobacco too. He
smokes all day like a kitchen chimney.

MIRANDA [*to* Clarinda].

    Prithee let's tease him a little. 'Tis the greatest pleasure
we have. —Morrow Uncle.

SNARL.

    How now, you baggages, what do you abroad thus early?   80
You us'd to be stewing a-bed till eleven a clock like paltry,

lazy cockatrices that are good for nothing, by the mass. You'll make excellent wives, cuckold your husbands immoderately. You mind nothing but prinking yourselves up. A wholesome, good, housewifely country wench is   85 worth a thousand of you, in sadness.

MIRANDA.

You have a coarse stomach, and to such a one a sirloin of beef were better than a dish of wheatears.

SNARL.

A man must have a lusty stomach that has a mind to any of the town ladies. They have so many tricks to disguise   90 themselves—washing, painting, patching, and their damn'd ugly, new-fashion'd dresses—that a man knows not what to make on 'em, by the mass. Besides, I have not heard that their reputations are famous all over the world?

CLARINDA.

You are an old-fashion'd fellow, uncle, and think no dress   95 handsome but that which ladies wore at the coronation of the last king.

MIRANDA.

And think no ladies honest but your old, formal creatures that were in fashion in the year 1640, and censure all ladies that have freedom in their carriage.   100

SNARL.

Freedom with a pox! Ay, 'tis freedom indeed. But the last age was an age of innocence. You young sluts you, now a company of jillflirts, flaunting, vain cockatrices, take more pains to lose reputation than those did to preserve it. I am afraid the next age will have very few that are lawfully be-   105 gotten in't, by the mass. Besides, the young fellows are like all to be effeminate coxcombs, and the young women, strumpets, in sadness, all strumpets, by the mass.

CLARINDA.

You are a fine old satyr indeed. 'Twere well if you decried vices for any other reason but that you are past them.   110

SNARL.

You pert baggages, you think you are very handsome now,

---

88. *wheatears*] small, tender northern birds.
96–97. *coronation . . . king*] Charles I was crowned on March 27, 1625.

I warrant you. What a devil's this pound of hair upon your
paltry frowses for? What a pox are those patches for? What,
are your faces fore? I'd not kiss a lady of this age; by the
mass, I'd rather kiss my horse.   115

MIRANDA.

Heav'n, for the general good of our sex, keep you still in
that mind.

SNARL.

Some ladies with scabs and pimples on their faces invented
patches, and those that have none must follow just as our
young fellows imitate the French. Their summer fashion of 120
going open-breasted came to us at Michaelmas, and we wore
it all winter. And their winter fashion of buttoning close
their straight, long-waisted coats that made them look like
monkeys came not to us till March, and our coxcombs wore
it all summer. Nay, I'll say that for your comfort the young, 125
fashionable fellows of the town have as little wit as you
have.

CLARINDA.

You had a better opinion of our sex sure in your youth.
Were you never in love?

MIRANDA.

O yes, with himself always.   130

SNARL.

Never with any such as you, I thank Heav'n. I was never
such an ass. I'd not be such a puppy for the world, in
sadness.

CLARINDA.

Pish. You are an old, insignificant fellow, nuncle, such as
you should be destroyed like drones that have lost their 135
stings and afford no honey.

SNARL.

Marry come up, you young slut. Are you liquorish after the
honey of man? In sadness, this is fine.

MIRANDA.

You have no pleasure but drinking, and smoking, and riding

113–114. What . . . fore?] *Q 1–3 have*   What. *The sentence could mean*
fore, *but only Q 1 shows a comma after*   "What are your faces for?"

---

113. *frowses*] wigs of frizzed hair worn by women. See III.iv.149.

with your gambadoes on your little pacing tit, to take a pipe, 140
and drink a cup of ale at Hampstead or Highgate.

SNARL.

Prithee, you prating slut, do not trouble me with your
impertinence. What pleasure can a man have in this
coxcombly, scandalous age? In sadness, I am almost
asham'd to live in't, by the mass.   145

CLARINDA.

Then die in it as soon as you can if you do not like it.

MIRANDA.

Methinks though all pleasures have left you, you may go
see plays.

SNARL.

I am not such a coxcomb, I thank God. I have seen 'em at
Blackfriars. Pox, they act like poppets now, in sadness. I 150
that have seen Joseph Taylor, and Lowin, and Swanstead!
O, a brave roaring fellow would make the house shake
again. Besides, I can never endure to see plays since women
came on the stage; boys are better by half.

Enter Snarl's *man [with a pipe].*

CLARINDA.

But here are a great many new plays.   155

SNARL.

New ones! Yes, either damn'd, insipid, dull farces, con-
founded toothless satires, or plaguy rhyming plays with

147–148. go see] *Q1;* go to see *Q2–3.*

---

140. *gambadoes*] large boots or gaiters, attached to the saddle to protect a
rider's legs from wet and cold.

140. *tit*] a small horse; often implying a nag.

150. *Blackfriars*] The second Blackfriars theater was built in 1596 and
demolished in 1655.

151. *Joseph Taylor . . . Swanstead*] "In the reign of Charles I John
Lowin and Joseph Taylor were the most widely known members of the
King's company, the recognized leaders of the organization." By 1624
Eyllaerdt Swanston (variously Swanstead) had become a member of the
King's company, and by 1633 he had probably begun to share the leading
roles with the ageing Taylor and Lowin. (Gerald Eades Bentley, *The
Jacobean and Caroline Stage* [Oxford, 1941], II, 499–506, 584–588, 590–598.
In the same volume, pp. 691–696, see "A Dialogue of Plays and Players"
[James Wright], *Historia Histrionica* [London, 1699]. All three players are
mentioned there prominently and together.)

scurvy heroes worse than the Knight of the Sun or Amadis
de Gaul, by the mass. Pish, why should I talk with such
foolish girls? —Here sirrah, give me my pipe of tobacco, 160
with the match. So— (*He smokes.*) Go now, and fetch
me a lusty tankard of ale with nutmeg and sugar in't.

[Exit Man.]

MIRANDA [*to* Clarinda].

Prithee do thee fling away his cane, and I'll break his pipe
which will almost break his heart.

CLARINDA.

Agreed. —Fie, nuncle, is this your breeding to take nasty 165
tobacco and stink much before ladies?

MIRANDA.

Away with it.

(Clarinda *flings away his cane;* Miranda *breaks his pipe.*)

SNARL.

'Sdeath! You fancy jades, what's this? I'll thrum you! 'Twas
well you flung away my cane, you young sluts; in sadness,
I'd ha' made bamboo fly about your jackets else, by the 170
mass. Ha, 'tis not broken all to pieces.

(*While he is stooping for his pipe, one flings away his hat and periwig, the
other thrusts him down.*)

'Ounds! You young jades, I'll maul you, you strumpets,
you damn'd cockatrices. I'll disinherit my nephew if he does
not turn you out of doors, you crocodiles.

CLARINDA.

That's it we'd have. We'll weary you both of your lives till 175
you bring it about.

SNARL.

You young jades, you strumpets!

Exit Snarl, *looking for his hat and periwig.*

---

158. *Knight of the Sun*] an ancestor of Amadis and hero of the romance
Knight of the Sun, Mirror of Princes and Knights by Diego Ortuñez de Calahorra
and Marcos Martinez, first printed at Saragossa in 1562. To this knight is
ascribed one of the prefatory poems in *Don Quixote.*

158–159. *Amadis de Gaul*] the title figure of a great prose-epic of feu-
dalism and chivalry, probably fourteenth century, Spanish or Portuguese,
author unknown though variously attributed.

MIRANDA.

Let's away. He'll beat us.

Enter Sir Formal.

SIR FORMAL.

Ladies, whither so gay and in such haste? Is Sir Nicholas
here?   180

MIRANDA.

No, no. Clarinda, come away.   [*Exit* Miranda.]

SIR FORMAL.

(*He lays hold on* Clarinda.)   Let me first violently ravish a
kiss from your fair hands. I had this morning, ere I went
out, tender'd you my service of this day had I not opin'd I
should too early have disturb'd your beauty. But, madam, 185
you ignore not that those venturous blossoms whose over-
hasty obedience to the early spring does anticipate the
proper season do often suffer from the injuries of severer
weather unless protected by the happy patronage of some
more benign shelter.   190

CLARINDA.

Farewell, I am in haste—   *Exit* Clarinda.

SIR FORMAL.

Her departure favors somewhat of abruptness.

Enter Snarl.

SNARL.

Strumpets, jades!

SIR FORMAL.

Sweet Mr. Snarl, had my eyes sooner encounter'd you, I had
more early paid you the tribute of my respect, which I 195
opine to be so much your due that though I ignore not
that you are happy in having many admirers, yet—

SNARL.

'Ounds, if I be not reveng'd on these cockatrices.

SIR FORMAL.

Yet I say, none of 'em is endu'd with a more zealous heart
to do you service than your most humble servant Sir Formal 200
Trifle.

198. these] *Q1;* those *Q2–3.*

SNARL.

Pox! What, do you trouble me with your foolish rhetoric?

SIR FORMAL.

What is it so disorders the operative faculties of your noble
soul? But I beseech you argue you me not of oratory
though I confess it to be a great virtue to be florid, nor is 205
there in the whole world so generous and prince-like a
quality as oratory—

SNARL.

Prince-like! Pimp-like, in sadness! I never knew an orator
that was not a rascal, by the mass. Orators are foolish,
flashy coxcombs, of no sense or judgment, turn'd with every 210
wind. They are never of the same opinion half an hour
together, nor ever speak of the opinion they are of. Pox o'
your tropes and flowers.

SIR FORMAL.

Sir, upon my honor you mistake me still. I assure you I am
a person—   215

SNARL.

Whom I hope to see hang'd.

SIR FORMAL.

O sir, you are in a merry humor. But in good earnest, there
is not a person in the whole world that is a greater admirer
of your politer parts than myself.

SNARL.

'Shaw! Pox of admirers, pish, what care I whether you be or 220
no. Prithee, pish, you are very troublesome, in sadness.

SIR FORMAL.

Well sir, you will have your pretty humors; you are dispos'd
to be merry.

SNARL.

Merry! O your Jack-pudding! Merry quoth a! 'Ounds, you
lie.   225

SIR FORMAL.

Sir, I have often intreated you to avoid passion. It drowns
your parts and obstructs the faculties of your mind while a
serene soul like that which I wear about me operates

220. 'Shaw!] Shaw! *Q1;* Pshaw!
Q2–3.

clearly, notwithstanding the oppression of clay and the
clog of my sordid, human body.   230
SNARL.

In sadness! Would you were hang'd that your serene soul
might be free from your sordid, human body. 'Tis a very
sordid one, by the mass.
SIR FORMAL.

O sir, I will retire and take away all occasions of your
uttering things that, *re vera*, are more injurious to yourself 235
than reflecting on me. I take my leave, sir.   *Exit.*
SNARL.

You do well in so doing, by the mass. It's a fine life I live
here. I am tormented with a couple of young, ramping sluts.
And then there's my nephew's wife, the most impertinent,
foolish creature breathing. Then my nephew is such a cox- 240
comb he has studied these twenty years about the nature of
lice, spiders, and insects and has been as long compiling a
book of geography for the world in the moon. Did he not
give me my board for nothing in hopes of my estate, I'd not
stay here. But above all villains and tedious, insipid block- 245
heads, this Sir Formal is the greatest; he is the most
intolerable plague I have. I could—

>   With any fools but orators dispense,
>   Who love words so, they never care for sense.   [*Exit.*]

ACT II

[II.i]
Enter Longvil, Bruce, *and* Sir Samuel *in the habit of Longvil's Footman.*

BRUCE.

We are here to our wishes, and neither the Virtuoso nor his
master of ceremonies within. If we could but meet with the
ladies now.
SIR SAMUEL.

Ay, if the ladies were but here you should see how I would

249. S.D.] *Q3; om. Q1–2.*

---

235. *re vera*] in truth.
240–243. *Then . . . moon*] See Introduction, p. xix.

show my parts. Whip slapdash. I'd come up roundly with   5
Miranda, faith boys, ha.

LONGVIL [*aside*].

A pox o' this fellow, he'll be intolerable. I see there's no
tampering with that edge tool call'd a fool.

SIR SAMUEL.

I am disguis'd cap-a-pie to all intents and purposes, and
if any man manages an *intriguo* better than I, I will never   10
hope for a masquerade more, or expect to dance myself
again into any lady's affection and about that business.
Come aloft, Sir Samuel, I say—

BRUCE.

But sweet Sir Samuel, if you discover yourself, you will be
turn'd out of the house and we for company.   15

SIR SAMUEL.

Let me alone. Pox, if I should be discover'd, I'll bring you
off as round as a hoop, in the twinkling of an oyster shell.
But Gad I cannot conceal myself from my mistress. My love
and wit will break out now and then a little about the edges
or I shall burst, faith and troth.   20

LONGVIL.

Yonder come the ladies. Good Sam, keep your distance.

SIR SAMUEL.

My distance! Why the ladies are by themselves. I'll present
you to 'em; I'll introduce you. Come along, pull away boys.
Now my choice lads. Hey poop, come aloft, boy, ha—

LONGVIL.

Do you hear, Sir Samuel, act the footman a little better, or   25
by Heav'n I'll turn you out of my livery.

SIR SAMUEL.

What a pox. You are upon the high ropes now. Prithee
Longvil, hold thy peace with a whipstitch, your nose in
my breech. I know what I have to do man. Do you think
to make a fool of pilgarlic?   30

LONGVIL.

By Heav'n pilgarlic, I'll cut your throat if you advance
beyond your post. Stand sentry there.

---

9. *cap-a-pie*] head to foot.
28. *whipstitch*] a running stitch in needlework; by transfer, expressing
sudden movement or action. (*OED* quotes this passage.)

BRUCE.

If you do not, Sam, you'll find your master very choleric, honest Sam.

SIR SAMUEL.

Choleric! What a pox care I? How shall I show my parts   35
about this business if I should stand here? Pshaw, prithee, hold thy peace—

Enter Clarinda *and* Miranda.

LONGVIL [*to* Sir Samuel].

Sirrah, stand there, and mind your waiting. Damn me, stand still.

SIR SAMUEL [*aside*].

What a pox does he mean now? O' my conscience and soul,   40
he has been a-drinking hard this morning, and is half seas over already.

LONGVIL.

Ladies, your humble servant.

BRUCE.

How long have we pray'd to Heav'n for this opportunity of kissing your hands.   45

CLARINDA.

I see then you can be devout upon some occasions.

LONGVIL.

We show'd our devotion sufficiently the first time we saw you; 'twas in a church, ladies.

MIRANDA.

Lord! That it should be our fortune to see you in a place so little us'd by you.   50

CLARINDA.

I warrant they came hither as they do to a playhouse, bolting out of some eating house, having nothing else to do in an idle afternoon.

MIRANDA.

'Tis a wonder they do not come as the sparks do to a play-house too, full of champagne, venting very much noise and   55
very little wit.

LONGVIL.

Whatever your intentions are, I am sure it is a very wicked thing for you to go to church.

MIRANDA.

How so, sir?

BRUCE.

Why to seduce zealous young men as we might have been   60
but for you.

CLARINDA.

Your zeal will never do you hurt, I warrant you.

LONGVIL.

You for your part committed sacrilege and robb'd Heav'n
of all my thoughts.

MIRANDA.

That's strange, for I assure you none of mine e'er stray'd   65
towards you.

LONGVIL.

I am glad to find you can be so very zealous. They that can
be so very violent in that higher sort of zeal will often be so
in a lower. I am glad to see my mistress violent in any
passion; 'tis ten to one love will have its turn then.   70

BRUCE.

You could not but observe my great zeal to you, madam.
Had I soar'd ne'er so high, you would have lured me down
again.

CLARINDA.

Alas, sir, you never soar so high, but any lure will bring
you down with a swoop, I warrant you.   75

MIRANDA.

You are he that have pester'd me with your *billets doux*,
your fine, little, fashionable notes tied with silk.

LONGVIL.

Yes, I have presented several bills of love upon you, and
you would never make good payment of any of 'em.

MIRANDA.

Would you have one answer a bill of love at sight? That's   80
only for substantial traders; young beginners dare not
venture, they ought to be cautious.

LONGVIL.

Not when they know him to be a responsible merchant they
have to deal with.

MIRANDA.

Such who keep a correspondence with too many factories,   85 venture too much, and are in danger of breaking.

CLARINDA.

My sister's in the right. 'Tis more danger trusting love
with such than money with goldsmiths; especially considering most men are apt to break in women's debts. I have
received several honorable summons from you if I would   90
have accepted the challenges.

BRUCE.

I only provok'd you fairly into the open field, and, 'gad, I
wonder you had not honor enough to answer me.

CLARINDA.

You would have drawn me into some wicked ambush or
other, matrimony or worse, I warrant you.   95

SIR SAMUEL [aside].

What a pox do these fellows mean? I shall stand here till
one of 'em has whipped away my mistress about business
with a *hixius doxius*, with the force of repartee, and this and
that, and everything in the world.

(*Offers to go to* Clarinda.)

LONGVIL [*to* Sir Samuel].

Why sirrah, rascal!   100

SIR SAMUEL.

Ay, 'tis no matter for that. —Madam—

(*Pulls* Miranda *by the sleeve.*)

LONGVIL.

You impudent dog.   (Longvil *kicks him.*)

SIR SAMUEL [*aside*].

Pshaw! Pshaw! I care not a farthing for this. This is nothing,
I am harden'd. I have been kill'd and beaten to all intents
and purposes an hundred times about intrigues and   105
businesses. —Madam, madam, don't you know me?

MIRANDA.

What impudent, saucy footman's this?

BRUCE.

Poor silly rogue, he must be beaten into good manners.

97. 'em] *Q 1, 3;* them *Q 2.*

98. *hixius doxius*] This is obviously made up, on the analogy of *hocus pocus.*

SIR SAMUEL [*aside*].

> Ha-ha-ha, that's good, i'faith! Poor silly rogue, that's well!
> Ha-ha-ha. But all these kicks and these businesses and all 110
> that, we men of intrigue must bear. —Prithee, Longvil,
> do not play the fool, but let me discover myself.

LONGVIL.

> Sirrah, be gone, or I'll beat you most infinitely. —Madam,
> let us not trifle away those few happy minutes fortune lends
> us lovers. We know your straits, and how few opportunities 115
> we are like to have; and therefore let me tell you in short,
> I am most desperately in love with you.

SIR SAMUEL [*aside*].

> O traitor! What says he? I must discover myself quickly
> about this business, or, whip-slap, I shall be bobb'd of my
> mistress in the twinkling of a bedstaff.   120

MIRANDA [*aside*].

> 'Tis true, our opportunities are like to be rare, but I'll
> improve this so well we shall need no more. —Good sir, let
> it not transport you too much; for I do assure you, I am
> extremely and desperately out of love with you, and shall
> be so as long as I live.   125

LONGVIL.

> Say you so, madam? And are you absolutely and violently
> resolv'd upon this?

MIRANDA.

> I am.

LONGVIL.

> Faith, madam, I am glad to hear on't. I never knew a
> woman absolutely resolve upon anything but she did the 130
> contrary.

BRUCE.

> I hope you'll not take example by your hardhearted sister
> to nip so hopeful a love in the bud, but nourish it, and in
> time 'twill bring forth fruit worth the gathering.

CLARINDA.

> It shall produce none for me; it's a dangerous, surfeiting fruit 135
> and I'll ha' none on't.

SIR SAMUEL [*aside*].

> I'll sing a song that I us'd to entertain 'em with, and that
> will discover me. I shall be even with these impudent fellows.
>
> (*Sings "She tripped like a barren doe, etc."*)

LONGVIL.

'Sdeath! What does this rascal mean?

BRUCE.

Pox on him. He sings worse than an old woman a-spinning. 140

CLARINDA.

How's this? I have heard that charming voice. 'Tis very like a coxcomb's that used to come hither, one Sir Samuel Hearty.

SIR SAMUEL [*aside*].

Peace, envy, peace, coxcomb! She never was so much in the wrong in her life. She was always malicious against me 145 because I could not love her, poor fool. Coxcomb, whipstitch, your nose in my breech, pish!

BRUCE.

Hang him, let him discover himself.

MIRANDA [*aside*].

'Tis he sure. What project's this? He was ever a great designer.   150

SIR SAMUEL.

I can hold no longer. —Madam, have you lost your senses?

LONGVIL.

'Sdeath! This rascal puts me beyond all patience. Impudent villain.   (*Kicks him.*)

SIR SAMUEL.

Ay, ay, it's no matter for that, it's no matter for that. I can 155 bear anything for my mistress. —Don't you know me yet?

CLARINDA [*aside*].

'Tis he. I'll make as if I did not know him, and we'll have excellent sport with him.

MIRANDA.

Hold, sir. By your favor, I am resolved to speak with him and know the meaning of this.   160

LONGVIL.

Sirrah.

SIR SAMUEL [*to* Longvil].

Pshaw! Prithee hold thy tongue. *Tace* is Latin for a candle, I say again.   [*Aside.*]   I knew I should screw her up to the

151. have you] *Q 1;* you have *Q 2–3.*
The sentence is interrogatory in all three
quartos.

tune of love. [*To* Miranda.]   Now do you know your
faithful servant Sir Samuel?   165

[Miranda *and* Sir Samuel *talk apart.*]

MIRANDA.

I do, but have a care. If my sister discovers you, you are
undone.

SIR SAMUEL.

I warrant you I'll be as secret as a cockle.

MIRANDA.

I am sorry you have been so exceedingly beaten and
kick'd, sir.   170

SIR SAMUEL.

Pshaw, pshaw, it's nothing, nothing. Come, come, 'tis well
it's no worse. Come, if any man in England outdoes me
in passive valor about intrigues, I am the son of a tinderbox.

MIRANDA.

Have a care, she suspects something.

SIR SAMUEL.

Ay, let me alone.   175

CLARINDA.

What saucy, impudent footman's this? Correct his
insolence and send him hence; I like not his face.

MIRANDA.

The truth is the rascal is saucy, but he'll learn better
manners.

SIR SAMUEL [*aside*].

Good. How the rogue's love makes her dissemble! A cunning 180
toad.

LONGVIL.

'Sdeath you dog! I'll learn you better manners. Get you
gone.   (*Kicks him.*)

SIR SAMUEL.

Pox on you. You overact a master and kick too hard about
business.   185

LONGVIL.

Do you hear, you nonsensical owl; be gone out of the garden,
or by Heav'n I'll run my sword in your guts.

BRUCE.

Hold, Longvil, do not kill him; 'twill be something uncivil.

188. him] *Q1, 3;* me *Q2.*

SIR SAMUEL.

Uncivil! What a pox do you talk? Uncivil! Why 'twill be
murder, man. Uncivil, quoth a— Well, I must be gone 190
with a cup of content to the tune of a damn'd beating, or
so— This is a fine, nimble piece of business that a man
cannot make love to his own mistress. But I'll come upon
him with a *Quare impedit* and a good, lusty cup of revenge
to boot.   *Exit* Sir Samuel. 195

CLARINDA.

We have discover'd your fool. Do you want a fool that
you must bring such a one as Sir Samuel along with you?

MIRANDA.

Perhaps they thought themselves not able to divert us and
brought him to assist them.

LONGVIL.

Faith, ladies, if you make trial of us if we be not able to 200
divert you, you shall find us very willing.

BRUCE.

I am sure if we do not divert you from your cruel resolutions,
we are the most undone men that ever sigh'd and look'd
pale for ladies, yet—

CLARINDA.

I do not doubt but some ladies, such as they are, may have 205
made you look pale and wan.

MIRANDA.

But a civil woman could never yet come near your hearts
or alter your faces.

LONGVIL.

The greatest generals do not 'scape always unwounded;
you have done my business, madam.   210

BRUCE.

I have held out a long time against the artillery of ladies'
eyes, but a random shot has maul'd me at last.

CLARINDA.

That cannot be. You were the greatest mutineers against
civil women that could be.

---

194. *Quare impedit*] a writ formerly in use directing a sheriff to command
a person to show cause "why he hinders."

MIRANDA.

> Always showing your parts against matrimony and de- 215
> fending the tawdry, ill-bred, fluttering wenches o' the
> town.

LONGVIL.

> That may be, madam, but we are taken off.

BRUCE.

> Ay, madam, we are taken off.

CLARINDA.

> There's no trusting you, for though you seem to be taken 220
> off, as you call it, yet you'll stick fast to your good old
> cause.

MIRANDA.

> A man often parts with his honesty but never with his
> opinion for a bribe.

> *Enter* Lady Gimcrack *and* Sir Samuel.

LADY GIMCRACK.

> Mr. Bruce and Mr. Longvil in the garden with my nieces 225
> say you? Young sluts! Do they snap at all the game that
> comes hither? What are they discoursing of?

SIR SAMUEL.

> Why to the tune of love, madam. What should young
> gentlemen and ladies talk of else?

LADY GIMCRACK.

> O impudent jillflirts! Cannot one young gentleman 'scape 230
> 'em? Are they making love to my nieces, say you?

SIR SAMUEL.

> Yes, that they are, madam, with a helter-skelter, whipdash,
> as round as a hoop; what should they do else? I'll retire.

> *Exit.*

LADY GIMCRACK.

> That's Mr. Bruce, a fine, straight, well-bred gentleman, of
> a pleasing form, with a charming air in his face. The other, 235
> Mr. Longvil, who has a pleasing sweetness in his counte-
> nance, an agreeable straightness, and a grateful composure
> and strength in his limbs. I am distracted in my choice on

224.1.] Lady Gimcrack and Sir Samuel talk apart; Sir Samuel departs, and Lady Gimcrack's presence is not noticed until line 247.

whom to fix my affection. Let me see, which shall I like
best? Mr. Bruce is a fine person really, and so is Mr. 240
Longvil; and so is Mr. Bruce I vow, and so is Mr. Longvil
I swear. In short, I like 'em both best, and these fluttering
sluts shall have none of 'em.

CLARINDA.

Prithee, sister, let's change our men, and then we shall be
troubled with no love from 'em.   245

MIRANDA.

Agreed. But if we be, it is shifting of our torment, and
that's some ease. But hold, we are undone; here's my
aunt.

LADY GIMCRACK.

Gentlemen, your servant. So, nieces, you are soon acquainted
with young gentlemen, I see. It will in modesty befit you 250
to retire.

LONGVIL.

We heard Sir Nicholas was at home and took the liberty
of a turn in the garden.

BRUCE.

Where by accident we found these ladies, who have done
us the honor to entertain some discourse with us.   255

LADY GIMCRACK.

They are always ready to show their little or no breeding.
You must pardon them; they are raw girls.

CLARINDA.

Thank Heav'n we have not had the age and experience of
your ladyship.

MIRANDA.

We will leave your reverend ladyship to show your great 260
wisdom and breeding.

LADY GIMCRACK.

How now, you pert sluts!   *Exeunt* Clarinda *and* Miranda.
—Gentlemen, you are not to take notice what these idle
girls say concerning my age, for I protest, gentlemen, I
exceed not twenty-two, upon my honor I do not.   265

LONGVIL [*to* Bruce].

That's well! I remember her a woman twenty years ago.

262. S.D.] *Q1–2; S.D. following l.*
261 Q3.

BRUCE [*to* Longvil].

> 'Tis true. [*To* Lady Gimcrack.] 'Tis impossible your
> ladyship should be more.

LONGVIL.

> You are in the very blossom of your age.

LADY GIMCRACK.

> O Lord, sirs, now, I swear, you do me too much honor. 270
> Yet had I not had some cares in the world and, the truth
> on't is, been married somewhat against my will, I might
> have look'd much better. But 'tis no matter for that, I am
> dispos'd of—

BRUCE [*to* Longvil].

> This is to let us know she does not care for her husband. 275

LONGVIL [*to* Bruce].

> She means to trust one or both of us.

LADY GIMCRACK.

> Yet I confess, Sir Nicholas is a fine, solitary, philosophical
> person. But my nature more affects the vigorous gaiety
> and jollity of youth than the fruitless speculations of age.

LONGVIL.

> Those fitter for your youth and blood. But may we not have 280
> the honor we were promis'd of seeing Sir Nicholas?

LADY GIMCRACK.

> The truth on't is, he is within but upon some private
> business. But nothing shall be reserved from such accom-
> plish'd persons are you are. The truth on't is, he's learning
> to swim. 285

LONGVIL.

> Is there any water hereabouts, madam?

LADY GIMCRACK.

> He does not learn to swim in the water, sir.

BRUCE.

> Not in the water, madam! How then?

LADY GIMCRACK.

> In his laboratory, a spacious room where all his instruments
> and fine knacks are. 290

LONGVIL.

> How is this possible?

267. S.D. *to* Longvil] (*Aside*) *Q 1–3.*   276. trust] *Q 2–3;* truss *Q 1.*

LADY GIMCRACK.

Why he has a swimming master comes to him.

BRUCE.

A swimming master! This is beyond all precedent. (*Aside.*)
He is the most curious coxcomb breathing.

LADY GIMCRACK.

He has a frog in a bowl of water, tied with a packthread by 295
the loins, which packthread Sir Nicholas holds in his teeth,
lying upon his belly on a table; and as the frog strikes, he
strikes; and his swimming master stands by to tell him
when he does well or ill.

LONGVIL [*aside*].

This is the rarest fop that ever was heard of.   300

BRUCE.

Few virtuosos can arrive to this pitch, madam. This is the
most curious invention I ever heard of.

LADY GIMCRACK.

Alas, he has many such. He is a rare mechanic philosopher.
The College indeed refus'd him. They envied him.

LONGVIL.

Were it not possible to have the favor of seeing this 305
experiment?

LADY GIMCRACK.

I cannot deny anything to such persons. I'll introduce you.

Exeunt.

[II.ii]

Scene opens and discovers Sir Nicholas *learning to swim upon a table;* Sir
Formal *and the* Swimming Master *standing by.*

SIR FORMAL.

In earnest this is very fine. I doubt not, sir, but in a short
space of time you will arrive at that curiosity in this
watery science that not a frog breathing will exceed you.
Though, I confess, it is the most curious of all amphibious
animals in the art, shall I say, or rather nature of swimming.   5

---

304. *College*] Gresham College, a title popularly given to the Royal
Society for the establishment that had preceded it. See Introduction, p. xvi.
[II.ii]

0.1.] On the swimming scene in general, see Introduction, pp. xxiv–xxv.

SWIMMING MASTER.

Ah, well struck, Sir Nicholas. That was admirable; that
was as well swum as any man in England can. Observe
the frog. Draw up your arms a little nearer, and then
thrust 'em out strongly. Gather up your legs a little more.
So. Very well. Incomparable.   10

Enter Bruce, Longvil, *and* Lady Gimcrack.

BRUCE.

Let's not interrupt them, madam, yet, but observe a little
this great curiosity.

LONGVIL.

'Tis a noble invention.

LADY GIMCRACK.

'Tis a thing the College never thought of.

SIR NICHOLAS.

Let me rest a little to respire. So, it is wonderful, my   15
noble friend, to observe the agility of this pretty animal
which, notwithstanding I impede its motion by the
detention of this filum or thread within my teeth which
makes a ligature about its loins, and though by many
sudden stops I cause the animal sometimes to sink or   20
immerge, yet with indefatigable activity it rises and keeps
almost its whole body upon the superficies or surface of this
humid element.

SIR FORMAL.

True, noble sir. Nor do I doubt but your genius will make
art equal if not exceed nature; nor will this or any other   25
frog upon the face of the earth outswim you.

SIR NICHOLAS.

Nay, I doubt not, sir, in a very little time to become
amphibious. A man by art may appropriate any element
to himself. You know a great many virtuosos that can
fly, but I am so much advanc'd in the art of flying that I can   30
already outfly that ponderous animal call'd a bustard, nor
should any greyhound in England catch me in the calmest

14. of] *Q1;* on *Q2–3.*

31. *bustard*] a genus of birds (*Otis*) remarkable for their great size and
running power.

day before I get upon wing. Nay, I doubt not but in a little
time to improve the art so far, 'twill be as common to buy
a pair of wings to fly to the world in the moon as to buy a   35
pair of wax boots to ride into Sussex with.

SIR FORMAL.

Nay, doubtless, sir, if you proceed in those swift gradations
you have hitherto prosper'd in, there will be no difficulty
in the noble enterprise, which is devoutly to be efflagitated
by all ingenious persons since the intelligence with that   40
lunary world would be of infinite advantage to us in the
improvement of our politics.

SIR NICHOLAS.

Right, for the moon being *domina humidiorum*, to wit the
governess of moist bodies, has, no doubt, the superior
government of all islands; and its influence is the cause   45
so many of us are delirious and lunatic in this. But having
sufficiently refrigerated my lungs by way of respiration, I
will return to my swimming.

SWIMMING MASTER.

Admirably well struck! Rarely swum! He shall swim with
any man in Europe.   50

SIR FORMAL.

Hold, Sir Nicholas. Here are those noble gentlemen and
philosophers whom I invited to kiss your hands. And I am
not a little proud of the honor of being the grateful and
happy instrument of the necessitude and familiar com-
munication which is like to intervene between such excellent   55
virtuosos.

BRUCE.

We are Sir Nicholas and your most humble servants.

LONGVIL.

We shall think ourselves much honored with the knowledge
of so celebrated a virtuoso.

---

39. efflagitated]   *Q1;*   effligated   43. *humidiorum*]   *Q2–3; humidorum*
Q2–3.   *Q1.*

33–36. *Nay . . . with.*] See Introduction, p. xix.

36. *wax boots*] waterproof boots of heavily waxed leather which were
worn in wet and marshy areas.

39. *efflagitated*] to demand or desire eagerly. (*OED* quotes this passage.)

SIR NICHOLAS.

You are right welcome into my poor laboratory. And if in   60
aught I can serve you in the way of science, my nature is
diffusive, and I shall be glad of communicating with such
eminent virtuosos as I am let to know you are.

LONGVIL.

We pretend to nothing more than to be your humble
admirers.   65

SIR FORMAL.

All the ingenious world are proud of Sir Nicholas for his
physico-mechanical excellencies.

SIR NICHOLAS.

I confess I have some felicity that way. But were I as
precelling in physico-mechanical investigations as you in
tropical rhetorical flourishes, I would yield to none.   70

LONGVIL [*aside*].

How the asses claw one another.

BRUCE.

We are both your admirers. But of all quaint inventions,
none ever came near this of swimming.

SIR FORMAL.

Truly I opine it to be a most compendious method that in a
fortnight's prosecution has advanc'd him to be the best   75
swimmer of Europe. Nay, it were possible to swim with any
fish of his inches.

LONGVIL.

Have you ever tried in the water, sir?

SIR NICHOLAS.

No, sir, but I swim most exquisitely on land.

BRUCE.

Do you intend to practice in the water, sir?   80

SIR NICHOLAS.

Never, sir. I hate the water. I never come upon the water,
sir.

LONGVIL.

Then there will be no use of swimming.

76. it were] *Q1;* if it were *Q2–3.*

_____

69. *precelling*] superior, surpassing.

SIR NICHOLAS.

I content myself with the speculative part of swimming;
I care not for the practic. I seldom bring anything to use;   85
'tis not my way. Knowledge is my ultimate end.

BRUCE.

You have reason, sir. Knowledge is like virtue, its own
reward.

SIR FORMAL.

To study for use is base and mercenary, below the serene
and quiet temper of a sedate philosopher.   90

SIR NICHOLAS.

You have hit it right, sir, I never studied anything for use
but physic, which I administer to poor people. You shall
see my method.

LONGVIL.

Sir, I beseech you, what new curiosities have you found out
in physic?   95

SIR NICHOLAS.

Why I have found out the use of respiration or breathing,
which is a motion of the thorax and the lungs whereby the
air is impell'd by the nose, mouth, and windpipe into the
lungs and thence expell'd farther to elaborate the blood
by refrigerating it and separating its fuliginous streams.   100

BRUCE [aside].

What a secret the rogue has found out!

SIR NICHOLAS.

I have found, too, that an animal may be preserv'd without
respiration when the windpipe's cut in two, by follicular

91. have] Q 1–2; om. Q 3.

96–100. Why . . . streams] Boyle, Hooke, and other members of the
Royal Society were experimenting upon respiration and artificial respiration. Lloyd points out that this passage is taken almost verbatim from a
review of a treatise of Swammerdam in Phil. Trans., October 21, 1667.

100. fuliginous] sooty; in the old physiology applied to certain thick
vapors or exhalations noxious to the head or other vital parts.

102–105. I . . . lungs] This passage reflects a very famous experiment
performed by Robert Hooke before the Royal Society, October 10, 1667,
on opening the thorax of a dog. After cutting away all the ribs and taking
out the diaphragm, Hooke blew with a pair of bellows into the windpipe;
as long as the bellows were used, the dog lived and breathed, but when the
bellows ceased, it became convulsive and dying. Hooke "remarked, that

impulsion of air: to wit, by blowing wind with a pair of
bellows into the lungs. 105

LONGVIL.

I have heard of a creature preserv'd by blowing wind in
the breech, sir.

SIR NICHOLAS.

That's frequent. Besides, though I confess I did not invent it,
I have perform'd admirable effects by transfusion of blood:
to wit, by putting the blood of one animal into another. 110

SIR FORMAL.

Upon my integrity, he has advanc'd transfusion to the acme
of perfection and has the ascendent over all the virtuosos
in point of that operation. I saw him do the most admirable
effects in the world upon two animals: the one a domestic
animal commonly call'd a mangy spaniel, and a less famelic 115
creature commonly call'd a sound bulldog. —Be pleas'd, sir,
to impart it.

SIR NICHOLAS.

Why I made, sir, both the animals to be emittent and
recipient at the same time. After I had made ligatures as
hard as I could (for fear of strangling the animals) to 120
render the jugular veins turgid, I open'd the carotid
arteries and jugular veins of both at one time, and so
caus'd them to change blood one with another.

SIR FORMAL.

Indeed that which ensu'd upon the operation was miraculous,
for the mangy spaniel became sound and the bulldog 125
mangy.

SIR NICHOLAS.

Not only so, gentlemen, but the spaniel became a bulldog
and the bulldog a spaniel.

SIR FORMAL.

Which considering the civil and ingenious temper and
education of the spaniel with the rough and untaught 130
savageness and ill-breeding of the bulldog, may not

---

he designed this experiment to understand the nature of respiration."
Reports are given in the minutes of the Royal Society for June 20, July 11,
1667 (also *passim*.): *Phil. Trans.*, II (1667), 539–540.

109. *transfusion of blood*] See Introduction, pp. xxii–xxiv.

115. *famelic*] pertaining to hunger, exciting hunger.

undeservedly challenge the name of a wonder.

BRUCE.

'Tis an experiment you'll deserve a statue for.

Enter Clarinda, Miranda, *and* Sir Samuel.

CLARINDA.

Sir, I must beg your pardon for my intrusion, but I have found out such a practice upon my sister as will nearly 135 concern you to prevent it.

SIR SAMUEL.

What does she mean now?

SIR NICHOLAS.

Against Miranda, say you?

CLARINDA.

This footman has brought a letter and has been tempting her from that vile man Sir Samuel Hearty. There 't is. 140

[Clarinda *hands the note to* Sir Nicholas.]

MIRANDA [*to* Sir Samuel].

'Tis no matter for her persecution. Be confident of me; you can endure anything.

SIR SAMUEL [*to* Miranda].

Ay, anything, the most substantial beating under the sun. I have had a pretty parcel o' kicks already about this business; but as long as I find love, I care not for kicking. 145

LONGVIL [*aside*].

A pox o' this rascal, he'll undo us.

SIR NICHOLAS.

This is a villain indeed to tempt my niece from that knight. Why he is a spark, a gallant, a wit o' th' town, the greatest debaucher of youth and corrupter of ladies in England.

SIR SAMUEL (*aside*).

The rogue has hit me to a cow's thumb. He's as cunning a 150 fellow as any is within forty shillings of his head.

SIR FORMAL.

The man indeed has spruce, polite, mercurial, and pretty, concise parts; but he's a little too volatile and flashy. He would make a fine person if he were but solid.

151. is] *Q1; om. Q2–3.*

---

150. *to . . . thumb*] exactly, perfectly, to a hair.

SIR SAMUEL [*aside*].

> Good! Solid! Would he so! That's as dull a fellow as a man 155
> would wish to lay his leg over.

LONGVIL.

> I confess he is my footman, but shall be no longer so. Let
> him be soundly pump'd and toss'd in a blanket.

SIR NICHOLAS.

> Truly it is an injury beyond all sufferance, and with your
> leave, I'll have him so exercis'd. Call in my people.   160

SIR SAMUEL.

> Hold, hold, sir! What do you mean! Sir Samuel desired me
> to deliver this note, and he's a person I am much beholden
> to. That's all I know o' th' matter: only that he is a fine
> gentleman and a witty, facetious person as any wears a head.

LONGVIL.

> Here! Where are my servants?   165

> *Enter Servants.*

> Sirrah! Strip that rascal's coat over his ears.

SIR SAMUEL.

> Hold, hold, Longvil! What, are you mad! I shall catch
> cold in the twinkling of a bedstaff, man.

SIR NICHOLAS.

> Do you hear: let him be taken, and first pumped soundly,
> and then toss'd in a blanket.   170

LONGVIL.

> Impudent rascal! Away with him.

MIRANDA.

> Pump him soundly, impudent fellow.

SIR SAMUEL (*aside*).

> Ah, my pretty little dissembling rogue.

SIR NICHOLAS.

> See it done to purpose, and then turn him out a doors.

SIR SAMUEL.

> What a devil shall I do? But she loves me still. Come, 'tis 175
> well it's no worse; my intrigue goes on rarely—

> *They hale him out.*

162. beholden] beholding *Q 1–3.*

---

158. *toss'd in a blanket*] Cf. *Mac Flecknoe*, l. 42: "The like was ne'er in
Epsom blankets toss'd."

CLARINDA.

Let's see the execution.

MIRANDA.

Come on, let's see how generously he suffers.

Exeunt Clarinda *and* Miranda.

SIR NICHOLAS.

But now to return to my transfusion.

LONGVIL.

That was a rare experiment of transfusing the blood of a 180
sheep into a madman.

SIR NICHOLAS.

Short of many of mine. I assure you I have transfus'd into a
human vein sixty-four ounces, avoirdupois weight, from
one sheep. The emittent sheep died under the operation,
but the recipient madman is still alive. He suffer'd some 185
disorder at first, the sheep's blood being heterogeneous,
but in a short time it became homogeneous with his own.

SIR FORMAL.

Ha. Gentlemen, was not this incomparable? But you shall
hear more.

Enter Snarl.

SIR NICHOLAS.

The patient from being maniacal or raging mad became 190
wholly ovine or sheepish: he bleated perpetually and chew'd
the cud; he had wool growing on him in great quantities;
and a Northamptonshire sheep's tail did soon emerge or
arise from his anus or human fundament.

SNARL.

In sadness, nephew, I am asham'd of you. You will never 195
leave lying and quacking with your transfusions and fool's
tricks. I believe if the blood of an ass were transfus'd into a
virtuoso, you would not know the emittent ass from the
recipient philosopher, by the mass.

SIR NICHOLAS.

O uncle, you'll have your way. He's a merry gentleman. 200

SNARL.

Pox! Merry! Prithee leave prating and lying. I am not
merry; I am angry with such coxcombs as you are.

SIR FORMAL.

> Well, sir, you are very pleasant and will have your facetious,
> pretty humors.

SNARL.

> You are the zany to this mountebank.   205

SIR NICHOLAS.

> Pray, uncle, interrupt us not. —To convince you, gentlemen,
> of the truth of what I say, here is a letter from the patient
> who calls himself the meanest of my flock and sent me some
> of his own wool. I shall shortly have a flock of 'em. I'll
> make all my clothes of 'em; 'tis finer than beaver. Here 210
> was one to thank me for the cure by sheep's blood just
> now.

SNARL.

> O yes. He did not speak, but bleated his thanks to you. In
> sadness, you deserve to be hang'd. You kill'd four or five
> that I know with your transfusion.   215

SIR NICHOLAS.

> Sir, alas, those men suffer'd not under the operation, but
> they were cacochymious and had deprav'd viscera, that is
> to say, their bowels were gangren'd.

SNARL.

> Pish! I do not know what you mean by your damn'd
> cacochymious canting, but they died, in sadness. Prithee 220
> make haste with your canting and lying, and let's go to
> dinner, or you shall quack by yourself.

LONGVIL.

> A pleasant, blunt old fellow.

BRUCE.

> He's in the wrong in abusing transfusion, for excellent
> experiments may be made in changing one creature into the 225
> nature of another.

LONGVIL.

> Nay, it may be improved to that height to alter the flesh of

220. canting] *Q1–2;* cantings *Q3.*

---

217. *cacochymious*] having unhealthy or depraved humors; in old medical
systems, unhealthy state of the body-fluids.

205. *zany*] a comic performer attending a clown or mountebank, who
imitates his master in a ludicrous fashion.

creatures that we eat, as much as grafting and inoculating does fruits.

SIR NICHOLAS.

'Tis very true; I do it; I use it to that end. 230

SNARL.

Pox! Let me see you invent anything so useful as a mouse-trap, and I'll believe some of your lies. Prithee, did not a fellow cheat thee with eggs which he pretended were laid with hairs in them, and you gave him ten shillings apiece for the eggs till I discover'd they were put in at a hole made 235 by a very fine needle.

SIR FORMAL.

Well Mr. Snarl, you have the prettiest way of drolling. —Gentlemen, pray let me recommend him to you; he's a fine, facetious, witty person indeed.

SNARL.

You recommend me! Prithee, damn'd orator, hold thy 240 tongue. In sadness, you are a foolish, flashy fellow.

BRUCE.

We shall be glad of the honor to know you.

SNARL.

I desire no acquaintance with any young man of this age, not I.

LONGVIL.

Why so, sir? 245

SNARL.

Why, they are vicious, illiterate, foolish fellows, good for nothing but to roar and make a noise in a playhouse; to be very brisk with pert whores in vizards, who, though never so ill-bred, are most commonly too hard for them at their own weapon: repartee. And when whores are not there, they 250 play monkey tricks with one another while all sober men laugh at them.

BRUCE.

They are even with them, for they laugh at all sober men again.

LONGVIL.

No man's happy but by comparison. 'Tis the great comfort 255

246. they] *Q1, 3;* then *Q2.*

of all the world to despise and laugh at one another.

SNARL.

But these are such unthinking animals and so weary of
themselves, they can never be alone, always complaining of
short life, yet never know what to do with the time they
have.   260

BRUCE.

This snarling fellow's sometimes in the right.

SNARL.

Their top of their education is to smatter French, for in
France they have been to learn French vices to spend
English estates with, with an insipid gaiety which is to be
slight and bright, very pert and very dull.   265

SIR NICHOLAS.

Sir, I beseech you be civiller to my friends.

SNARL.

I am transported with passion against the young fellows of
the age.

LONGVIL.

Old fools always envy young fools.

SNARL.

They are all forward and positive in things they understand 270
not; they laugh at any gentleman that has art or science;
and make it the property of a well-bred gentleman to be
good for nothing, but to make a figure in the drawing room,
set his periwig in the glass, smile, whisper, and make legs
and foolish faces for an hour or two without one word of 275
sense, in sadness.

BRUCE.

The snarling rogue's very tart upon the youngsters.

LONGVIL.

When the pleasures of wine and women, the joys of youth,
leave us, envy and malice, the lusts of age, succeed 'em.

SNARL.

Besides, they are all such whoring fellows, in sadness, I am 280
asham'd of 'em. The last age was an age of modesty.

262. Their] *Q1–2;* The *Q3.*   281. an age] *Q1–2;* the age *Q3.*
266. you be] *Q1;* you to be *Q2–3.*

BRUCE.

> I believe there was the same wenching then; only they
> dissembled it. They added hypocrisy to fornication, and so
> made two sins of what we make but one.

LONGVIL [*to* Bruce].

> After all his virtue, this old fellow keeps a whore. I'll tell 285
> you more on't.

SIR NICHOLAS.

> I hope you'll pardon the rough nature of my uncle, who
> spares nobody. Now if you please, gentlemen, we'll retire. I
> am sorry I cannot perform the dissection of the lobster,
> which I promis'd. My fishmonger that serves me for that 290
> operation has fail'd me; but I'll assure you it is the most
> curious of all testaceous or crustaceous animals whatsoever.

SIR FORMAL.

> But we will read an author and sport about a little Greek
> and Latin before dinner. The one is a noble refection of the
> mind as the other is of the body. 295

LONGVIL.

> We wait on you.

SIR NICHOLAS.

> After dinner we will have a lecture concerning the nature
> of insects and will survey my microscopes, telescopes,
> thermometers, barometers, pneumatic engines, stentro-
> phonical tubes, and the like. 300

BRUCE.

> We are infinitely oblig'd to you, sir. [*To* Longvil.] But
> all this does not edify with our mistresses, Longvil.

LONGVIL [*to* Bruce].

> We must find a way to get rid of these insipid fools; I have a
> way to get rid of the lady.

SIR FORMAL.

> Gentlemen, we most humbly attend your motions. 305

BRUCE.

> We wait on you. *Exeunt omnes.*

---

294. *refection*] refreshment.
299–300. *stentrophonical tubes*] *Tuba Stentrophonica,* the name given by
Samuel Morland to the speaking-trumpet invented by him in 1671.
302. *edify*] prosper, achieve success.

ACT III

[III.i]   *Enter* Longvil *and* Miranda.

LONGVIL.

Dear madam, tender the life and welfare of a poor, humble lover.

MIRANDA.

What! A fashionable gentleman of this age and a lover! It is impossible. They are all keepers, and transplant tawdry things from the Exchange or the playhouse, and make the 5
poor creatures run mad with the extremity of the alteration, as a young heir being kept short does at the death of his father.

LONGVIL.

I was never one of those, madam; nothing but age and impotence can reduce me to that condition. I had rather 10
kill my own game than send to a poulterer's. Besides, I never eat tame things when wild of the same kind are in season. I hate your coop'd, cramp'd lady; I love 'em as they go about, as I do your barndoor fowl.

MIRANDA.

'Tis more natural indeed.   15

LONGVIL.

But had I been ne'er so wicked, you have made such an absolute whining convert of me that, forgetting all shame and reproach from the wits and debauchees of the town, I can be a martyr for matrimony.

MIRANDA.

Lord! That you should not take warning! Have not several 20
of your married friends, like those upon the ladder, bidden all good people take warning by them.

LONGVIL.

For all that, neither lovers nor malefactors can take it: one will make experiment of marriage and th'other of hanging, at their own sad costs. Neither of the executions will 25
e'er be left off.

---

21. *upon the ladder*] at the gallows.

MIRANDA.

> They are both so terrible to women, 'tis hard to know which to choose.

LONGVIL.

> If you ladies were willing, we men are apt to be civil upon easier terms.   30

MIRANDA.

> No, those terms are harder than the other.

LONGVIL.

> You are so nimble a man knows not which way to catch you.

MIRANDA.

> Once for all I assure you, I will never be catch'd any way by you.

LONGVIL.

> Do not provoke love thus, lest he should revenge his cause   35
> and make you dote upon some nauseous coxcomb whom all the town scorns.

MIRANDA.

> Let love do what it will, I neither dare nor will talk on't any longer.

LONGVIL.

> You are afraid of talking of love as some are of reading in a   40
> conjuring book, for fear it should raise the devil.

MIRANDA.

> Whatever you can say will as soon raise one as the other in me. But I must take leave of you and your similes. My uncle will want you.

LONGVIL.

> Will you not in charity afford me one interview more this   45
> afternoon?

MIRANDA.

> Provided I hear not one word of love and my uncle and aunt be secure. I shall be in the walk on the east side of the garden an hour hence. (*Aside.*) But, by your leave, I shall meet another there.   *Exit* Miranda.   50

LONGVIL.

> A thousand thanks for the honor. —Yonder comes Bruce and Clarinda. I'll retire.   *Exit* Longvil.

Enter Bruce *and* Clarinda.

BRUCE.

I have taken more pains to single you out than ever woodman did for a deer.

CLARINDA.

If the woodman were no better a marksman, the deer   55
would be safe for all his singling. Besides, I am not so
tame to stand a shot yet, I thank you.

BRUCE.

Lovers are quick aimers and can shoot flying.

CLARINDA.

Not if they fly so fast as I shall from you.

BRUCE.

Come, I see this way will not do; I'll try another with you.   60
Ah, madam, change your cruel intentions, or I shall become
the most desolate lover that ever yet, with arms across,
sigh'd to a murmuring grove or to a purling stream com-
plain'd. Savage I'll wander up and down the woods and
carve my passion on the barks of trees and vent my grief   65
to winds that as they fly shall sigh and pity me.

CLARINDA.

How now! What foolish fustian's this? You talk like an
heroic poet.

BRUCE.

Since the common, downright way of speaking sense would
not please you, I had a mind to try what the romantic way   70
of whining love could do.

CLARINDA.

No more of this. I had rather hear the tattling of gossips at
an upsitting or christening, nay, a fanatic sermon, or, which
is worse than all, a dull rhyming play with nothing in't but
lewd heroes huffing against the gods.   75

BRUCE.

Why, I'll try any sort of love to please you, madam. I'll
show you that of a gay coxcomb: with his full plumes,
strutting and rustling about his mistress like a turkey-cock,

71. whining] *Q1;* wining *Q2;*
winning *Q3.*

---

73. *upsitting*] the occasion of a woman's first sitting up to receive company
after confinement.

baiting her with brisk, airy motion and fashionable nonsense; thinking to carry her by dint of periwig and garniture   80
or by chanting some pretty, foolish sonnet of Phyllis and
Celia; or, at best, treating her with nothing but ends of
plays or second-hand jests which he runs on tick with witty
men for and is never able to pay them again.

CLARINDA.

No, there are too many of these fine sparks you talk of who   85
perhaps may be very clinquant, slight, and bright and
make a very pretty show at first, but the tinsel-gentlemen
do so tarnish in the wearing, there's no enduring them.

BRUCE.

But I am of good metal, madam, and so true that I shall
abide any touchstone, even that of marriage.   90

CLARINDA.

But it's an ill bargain where I must buy my metal first and
touch it afterwards.

BRUCE.

You shall touch it first, madam, and if you do not like it,
I'll take it again, and no harm done.

CLARINDA.

No, I'll take care there shall be no harm done. Pray divert   95
this unseasonable discourse of love, for I will never hear
on't more. Farewell. I see my Lady Gimcrack in the garden.

BRUCE.

Let me but beg to have one treaty more with you this afternoon. If I convince you not of the error of your hard heart,
I must submit and be miserable.   100

CLARINDA.

If you love to hear the same thing again, I will declare it to
you an hour hence in the green walk on the other side the
wilderness. Farewell. [*Aside.*]   But, by your leave, you
shall find another in my place.   *Exit* Clarinda.

Enter Lady Gimcrack *at another door.*

BRUCE.

Your ladyship's humble servant. I have been taking the 105
fresh air in the garden, madam.

---

83. *tick*] credit, short for ticket.
86. *clinquant*] glittering with gold or silver; tinseled.

LADY GIMCRACK.

I am come with the same intention and am happy in the company of a person who is so much a gentleman.

BRUCE.

Your ladyship does me too much honor.

LADY GIMCRACK.

By no means, sir; your accomplishments command respect 110 from all ladies. I doubt not but you have been happy in many ladies' affections.

BRUCE (aside).

What will this come to?

LADY GIMCRACK.

But women will be frail while there are such persons in the world: that's most certain.   115

BRUCE.

Your ladyship's in a merry humor to rally a poor young gentleman thus.

LADY GIMCRACK.

Far be it from me, I swear. Your perfections are so prevalent that were I not in honor engag'd unto Sir Nicholas (and honor has the greatest ascendant in the world upon me), I 120 assure you I would not venture myself alone with such a person; but honor's a great matter, a great thing, I'll vow and swear.

BRUCE.

You ladies will abuse your humble servants; we are born to suffer.   125

LADY GIMCRACK.

Lord, sir, that you should take me to be in jest! I swear I am in earnest. And were I not sure of my honor, that never fail'd me in a doubtful occasion, I would not give you this opportunity of tempting my frailty; not but that my virtuous inclinations are equal with any ladies', but there 130 is a prodigious witchcraft in opportunity. But honor does much. Yet opportunity is a great thing, I swear, a great thing.

BRUCE.

Ay, madam, if we use it when it offers itself.

LADY GIMCRACK.

How sir! Ne'er hope for't! Ne'er think on't! I would not 135 for all the world, I protest. Let not such thoughts of me enter into your head. My honor will protect me. I make use of an opportunity! I am none of those, I assure you.

BRUCE [*aside*].

'Sdeath! How apprehensive she is. I shall forget the speculative part of love with Clarinda and fall to the 140 practic with her. But I shall ne'er hold out that long journey without this or some other bait by the way.

LADY GIMCRACK.

Yet, as I was saying, opportunity's a bewitching thing. Let all ladies beware of opportunity I say. For alas, if we were not innocent and virtuous now, what use might we 145 make of this opportunity now.

BRUCE (*aside*.)

She's so damnably affected and silly 'twould pall anyone's appetite but mine. Folly and affection are as nauseous as deformity.

LADY GIMCRACK.

Should we now retire into that cool grotto for refresh- 150 ment, the censorious world might think it strange. But honor will preserve me. Honor's a rare thing, I swear. I defy temptation.

BRUCE.

You'll not give a man leave to trouble you with much. I have not observ'd that grotto. Shall I wait on you to survey it? 155

LADY GIMCRACK.

Ay, sir, with all my heart to survey that. But if you have any wicked intentions, I'll swear you'll move me pro- digiously. If your intentions be dishonorable, you'll provoke me strangely.

BRUCE.

Try me, madam. 160

LADY GIMCRACK.

Hold, hold, have a care what you do. I will not try if you be not sure of your honor. I'll not venture, I protest.

BRUCE.

Whatever you are of mine, you are sure of your own.

LADY GIMCRACK.

Right, that will defend me. Now tempt what you will.

---

148. *affection*] *affectation*.

Though we go in, nay, though we shut the door too, I fear 165
nothing. It's all one to me as long as I have my honor about
me. Come.

BRUCE.

Yonder comes Longvil, madam.

LADY GIMCRACK.

For Heav'n's sake remove from me, or he'll suspect my
honor.   170

BRUCE [*aside*].

So, this accident has preserv'd me honest. I am as constant
a lover as any man in England—when I have no opportunity to be otherwise.   *Exit* Bruce.

Enter Longvil.

LADY GIMCRACK.

Fa-la-la-la! O me, sir! I swear you frighted me. I protest
my heart was at my mouth. Alas, I shall not recover the 175
disorder a good while.

LONGVIL.

What's the matter, madam?

LADY GIMCRACK.

You brought a gentleman that's dead so fresh into my mind,
one that was the first object of my vows and affections, not
expecting to see you here. I vow I thought it had been his 180
ghost, upon my word.

LONGVIL.

I am happy in resembling anyone you could love, madam.

LADY GIMCRACK.

I have long forgotten my passion for him, but the sight of
you did stir in me a strange *je ne sais quoi* towards you; and
but that I am another's now—otherwise—But I say too 185
much.

LONGVIL (*aside.*)

I have been too much acquainted with her character to
doubt her meaning. —Madam, you honor me so much I
cannot acknowledge it enough by my words. My hearty
actions shall speak my thanks.   190

LADY GIMCRACK.

Actions! O Heav'n, what actions? I hope you mean

honorably. I swear you brought all the blood of my body
into my face. Actions, said you! I hope you are a person of
honor; my honor's dearer to me than the whole world. I
would not violate my reputation for the whole earth.   195

LONGVIL.

Let us retire, madam. If I do not show myself a man of
honor, may your ladyship renounce me.

LADY GIMCRACK.

Retire! Heav'n forbid! Are we not private enough? Well,
you put me more and more in mind of my first love, I swear
you do.   200

LONGVIL [*aside*].

By your leave, Miranda, I can hold no longer. Though I
am as true as steel, any handsome woman will strike fire on
me. —Let us repose a while in the grotto, madam.

LADY GIMCRACK.

O Heav'n, sir, do not tempt me. What, give myself an
opportunity! Consider my honor, sir; I am another's.   205

LONGVIL.

And shall be so still, madam. Whatsoever use I shall make
of your ladyship, I shall return you again and ne'er alter
the property. Dear madam, retire.

LADY GIMCRACK.

O Lord, sir, what do you mean? You fright me so I protest
my heart is at my mouth. I am no such person. Dear sir,   210
mistake me not, misconstrue not my freedom; I would not
for the world— Well, I swear you are to blame now; never
stir you are— But 'tis your first fault; I can forgive you.

LONGVIL.

I am sorry I have offended. But let us retire into the grotto,
and I'll make as many acknowledgments as I can.   215

LADY GIMCRACK.

Well, sir, since you are a little more civil, I am content for
discourse sake, for I love discourse mightily.

LONGVIL [*aside*].

Well, I am a rogue. Dear Miranda, forgive me this once.
—Come, dear madam.

192. of] *Q 1–2;* in *Q 3.*
194. world] *Q 1, 3;* word *Q 2.*

LADY GIMCRACK.

I'll follow. But d' ye hear, sir, if you be the least uncivil, upon 220
my honor I'll cry out. Remember, sir, I give you warning.
Do not think on't; I swear and vow I will; do not, I say,
do not.

LONGVIL.

No, no, I warrant you. I'll trust you for that. (*Aside.*)
How fearful she is I should not think on't. 225

Enter Sir Formal.

SIR FORMAL.

Sweet Mr. Longvil, Sir Nicholas Gimcrack desires your
noble presence: he being now ready to impart those secrets
about insects which I dare be bold to say no virtuoso,
domestic or foreign, has explor'd but himself.

LONGVIL.

I wait on you. 230

SIR FORMAL.

I humbly kiss your ladyship's fair hands.

Exeunt Longvil *and* Sir Formal.

LADY GIMCRACK.

Shame on this unlucky fellow. I have discover'd the cross
love between my nieces and these gentlemen and will make
work with it.

Enter Maid *to* Lady Gimcrack.

MAID.

Madam, here's a letter for your ladyship. The messenger 235
would deliver it to none but me. [*Exit.*]

LADY GIMCRACK.

Ha! It is from my dear Hazard. (*Reads.*) "Madam, I
am extremely impatient to see your ladyship at the old place
of assignation as well for a great deal of love as for a little
business." Well, I will go though it cost me money. I know 240
that's his little business. I know not why we ladies should
not keep as well as men sometimes. But I shall neglect my
important affair with these two fine, sweet persons; but
that's uncertain, this is sure. *Exit.*

[III.ii]   *Enter* Snarl *and* Mrs. Figgup.

SNARL.

How happy am I in thy love! Here I can find retreat
when tir'd with all the rogues and fools in town.

MRS. FIGGUP.

Ay, dearest, come to thine own miss; she loves thee, buddy,
poor buddy. Coachee, coachee.

SNARL.

O my poor rogue. But when didst thou see thy friend Mrs.   5
Flirt, my nephew Gimcrack's mistress?

MRS. FIGGUP.

O shame on her! Out upon her! O name her not!

SNARL.

Why, what's the matter, bird?

MRS. FIGGUP.

O filthy creature. I cannot abide her. She's nought, she's
nought.   10

SNARL.

Why, what's the matter, Figg? What has she done to thee?

MRS. FIGGUP.

Done! I'll never forgive her while I ha' breath. Do not speak
of her; she's a base creature. Name her not; I ha' done
with her.

SNARL.

Has she affronted thee, poor rogue? I'll have her maul'd.   15
Filthy creature.

MRS. FIGGUP.

Ay, bird's-nie, she's a quean. But do not thee trouble thyself
with her; 'tis no matter.

SNARL.

I will know what she has done to thee. In sadness, if you
do not tell me, I won't love thee, pig's-nie.   20

MRS. FIGGUP.

Well, I will, but won't you laugh at me then?

0.1.] *scene division om.* Q *1–3.*   naught . . . naught Q *2–3.*
9–10. nought . . . nought] Q *1;*

---

17. *bird's-nie*] an obsolete vulgar term of endearment; cf. *pig's-nie*, 1. 20
17. *quean*] prostitute.
20. *pig's-nie*] another vulgar term of endearment.

SNARL.

No, by the mass, not I.

MRS. FIGGUP.

Nay, but thou wilt, bird.

SNARL.

In sadness, I won't.

MRS. FIGGUP.

Why, would you think it? I wish I might ne'er stir out o'   25
this place if the lewd carrion had not the impudence to
tell me that Sir Nicholas Gimcrack was a handsomer man
than thou art. No, I'll ne'er forgive her while I ha' breath.

SNARL.

Poor rogue, thou art a dear creature, in sadness.

MRS. FIGGUP.

Impudent flirts! But I swear our sex grows so vicious and   30
infamous I am asham'd of 'em; they have no modesty in
'em.

SNARL.

In sadness, it's a very wicked age; men make no conscience o' their ways, by the mass. In the last age we were
modest and virtuous; we spent our time in making visits   35
and playing at cards with the ladies—so civil, so virtuous,
and well-bred.

MRS. FIGGUP.

For my part, I blush at the impudent creatures of the
town. That's the truth on't.

SNARL.

So do I, in sadness. To see villains wrong their sweet wives,   40
and, while they keep them short, let little dowdy strumpets
spend their estates for 'em. By the mass, my heart bleeds to
see so great a decay of conjugal affection in the nation.

MRS. FIGGUP.

Out upon 'em, filthy wenches. I wonder they dare show
their harden'd faces. They are so bold 'tis a burning shame   45
they should be suffer'd, I vow.

SNARL.

Nay, the young coxcombs are worse: nothing but swearing,
drinking, whoring, tearing, ranting, and roaring. In
sadness, I should be weary of the world for the vices of it
but that thou comfortest me sometimes, buddy.   50

MRS. FIGGUP.

Prithee dear numps, talk no more of 'em. I spit at 'em, but I
love n'own buddy man. Perdie, kiss me.

SNARL.

Ah poor budd, poor rogue, we are civil now. What harm's in
this?

MRS. FIGGUP.

None, none. Poor dear, kiss again, man.   55

SNARL.

Ah poor thing. In sadness, thou shalt have this purse; nay,
by the mass, thou shalt.

MRS. FIGGUP.

Nay pish, I cannot abide the money, not I. I love thee;
thou art a civil, discreet, sober person of the last age.

SNARL.

Ah poor little rogue. In sadness, I'll bite thee by the lip,   60
i'faith I will. Thou has incens'st me strangely; thou hast
fir'd my blood; I can bear it no longer, i'faith I cannot.
Where are the instruments of our pleasure? Nay, prithee
do not frown; by the mass, thou shalt do't now.

MRS. FIGGUP.

I wonder that should please you so much that pleases me so   65
little.

SNARL.

I was so us'd to't at Westminster School I could never
leave it off since.

MRS. FIGGUP.

Well, look under the carpet then if I must.

SNARL.

Very well, my dear rogue. But dost hear, thou art too gentle. 70
Do not spare thy pains. I love castigation mightily. So
here's good provision.

> *Pulls the carpet; three or four great rods fall down.*

[VOICES] *within.*

Ho there within! Open the door. 'Sdeath, I'll break it

52. Perdie] Predee *Q 1–3.*

---

52. *Perdie*] by God.
69. *carpet*] wall hanging.
73. S.P. [*Voices*] *within.*] Mrs. Figgup's brother and his servants or
friends; they do not appear onstage at any time.

open. What rascal have you got with you? I'll maul
him.   75

MRS. FIGGUP [aside].

O Heav'n, this rascal will undo me. What shall I do? —'Tis
my brother.

SNARL.

In sadness, I shall be ruin'd.

MRS. FIGGUP.

Run, run, if you love me, into the woodhole quickly. I'll
get rid of him. For Heav'n's sake take the birch along with   80
you.

SNARL.

Ah hectoring rascal! We had none o' this in the last age.
Rogues! Dogs! A man cannot be in a private with a sister,
but he must be disturb'd by th' impertinent brother, in
sadness.   85

MRS. FIGGUP.

In! In! I'll out to him.   *Exeunt.*

[III.iii]

       Sir Nicholas, Sir Formal, Bruce, Longvil [*are onstage*].

SIR FORMAL.

I do assure you, gentlemen, no man upon the face of the
earth is so well seen in the nature of ants, flies, humble-bees,
earwigs, millepedes, hog's lice, maggots, mites in a cheese,
tadpoles, worms, newts, spiders, and all the noble products
of the sun by equivocal generation.   5

SIR NICHOLAS.

Indeed, I ha' found more curious phenomena in these
minute animals than in those of vaster magnitude.

LONGVIL.

I take the ant to be a most curious animal.

0.1.] *scene division om. Q 1–3.*

---

2. *humble-bees*] bumble-bees; the older word is still extant.

5. *equivocal generation*] the (supposed) production of plants or animals
without parents; spontaneous generation.

6–11. *Indeed . . .filemot.*] Lloyd points out that the technical description
of the ants in this passage is very close to one submitted by Dr. King to the
Phil. Trans., May 11, 1667.

SIR NICHOLAS.

    More curious than all oviparous, or egg-laying, creatures
in the whole world. There are three sorts: black, dark brown,   10
and filemot.

LONGVIL.

    Right, sir.

SIR NICHOLAS.

    The black will pinch the dark brown with his forceps till
it kills it upon the place; the like will the dark brown do
by the filemot. I have dissected their eggs upon the object   15
plate of a microscope, and find that each has within it an
included ant, which has adhering to its anus, or fundament,
a small black speck, which becomes a vermicle, like a mite,
which I have watch'd whole days and nights. And Sir
Formal has watch'd 'em thirty hours together.   20

LONGVIL.

    A very pretty employment.

SIR FORMAL.

    And a long time we could find no motion but that of
flexion and extension, but at last it becomes an ant,
gentlemen.

BRUCE.

    What does it concern a man to know the nature of an ant?   25

LONGVIL.

    O it concerns a virtuoso mightily; so it be knowledge, 'tis
no matter of what.

BRUCE.

    Sir, I take 'em to be the most politic of all insects.

SIR FORMAL.

    You have hit it, gentlemen. They have the best govern-
ment in the world. What do you opine it to be?   30

LONGVIL.

    O, a commonwealth most certainly.

SIR NICHOLAS.

    Worthy sir, I see you are a great observer; it is a republic

---

11. *filemot*] a color like that of dead or faded leaves.

28–35. *Sir . . . animals.*] The democratic government of the ants is
satire upon the political experiment of the Commonwealth, as well as
upon the government of Holland and the scientific super-efficiency of the
Dutch. See Introduction, p. xxvi.

resembling that of the States General.

BRUCE.

Undoubtedly. And the Dutch are just such industrious and
busy animals.   35

SIR FORMAL.

Right. But now I beseech you be pleas'd to communicate
some of your quainter observations to these philosophers
about those subtle and insidious animals call'd spiders.

SIR NICHOLAS.

I think I have found out more phenomena or appearances
of nature in spiders than any man breathing. Would you   40
think it: there are in England six and thirty several sorts of
spiders; there's your hound, greyhound, lurcher, spaniel
spider.

LONGVIL.

But above all, your tumbler spider is most admirable.

SIR NICHOLAS.

O sir, I am no stranger to't. It catches flies as tumblers do   45
conies.

BRUCE [to Longvil].

Good! How these fools will meet a lie halfway.

LONGVIL [to Bruce].

Great liars are always civil in that point. As there is no lie
too great for their telling, so there's none too great for their
believing.   50

SIR NICHOLAS.

The fabric or structure of this insect with its texture is most
admirable.

SIR FORMAL.

Nor is its sagacity or address less to be wonder'd at, as I
have had the honor to observe under my noble friend. As
soon as it has spied its prey, as suppose upon a table, it will   55
crawl underneath till it arrive to the antipodes of the fly
which it discovers by sometimes peeping up; and if the
capricious fly happens not to remove itself by crural motion
or the vibration of its wings, it makes a fatal leap upon the
heedless prey, of which, when it has satisfied its appetite, it   60
carries the remainder to its cell or hermitage.

---

42. *lurcher*] a mongrel breed of dogs, often used by poachers.
58. *crural*] of or belonging to the leg. (*OED* quotes this passage.)

SIR NICHOLAS.

It will teach its young ones to hunt and discipline 'em
severely when they commit faults. And when an old one
misses its prey, it will retire and keep its chamber for grief,
shame, and anguish ten hours together. 65

SIR FORMAL.

Upon my integrity it is true, for I have several times, by
Sir Nicholas' command, watch'd the animal upon this or
the like miscarriages.

SIR NICHOLAS.

But, sir, there is not in the world a more docible creature;
I have kept several of 'em tame. 70

BRUCE.

That's curious indeed. I never heard of a tame spider
before.

SIR NICHOLAS.

One above all the rest; I had call'd him Nick, and he
knew his name so well he would follow me all over the
house. I fed him indeed with fair flesh flies. He was the 75
best natur'd, best condition'd spider that ever I met with.
You knew Nick very well, Sir Formal; he was of the spaniel
breed, sir.

SIR FORMAL.

Knew him! I knew Nick intimately well.

LONGVIL [to Bruce].

These fools are beyond all that art or nature e'er produc'd. 80

BRUCE [to Longvil].

These are the admirable secrets they find out.

LONGVIL.

Have you observ'd that delicate spider call'd tarantula?

SIR NICHOLAS.

Now you have hit me; now you come home to me. Why I
travel'd all over Italy and had no other affair in the world
but to study the secrets of that harmonious insect. 85

BRUCE.

Did you not observe the wisdom, policies, and customs of
that ingenuous people?

71. That's] *Q 2–3;* That *Q 1.*

---

69. *docible*] teachable; docile.

SIR NICHOLAS.

O by no means! 'Tis below a virtuoso to trouble himself
with men and manners. I study insects, and I have observ'd
the tarantula does infinitely delight in music, which is the   90
reason of its poison being drawn out by it. There's your
phenomenon of sympathy!

LONGVIL.

Does a tarantula delight so in music?

SIR NICHOLAS.

O extravagantly. There are three sorts: black, grey, and
red, that delight in three several sorts and modes of music.   95

BRUCE.

That was a curious inquisition. How did you make it?

SIR NICHOLAS.

Why I put them upon three several chips in water; then
caus'd a musician to play, first a grave pavan or allemande,
at which the black tarantula only mov'd. It danc'd to it
with a kind of grave motion much like the benchers at the   100
revels.

Enter Servant.

SERVANT.

Sir, the gentleman that's going for Lapland, Russia, and
those parts is come for your letters and queries which you
are to send thither.

SIR NICHOLAS.

I'll wait on him.   [*Exit* Servant.] 105
—I keep a constant correspondence with all the virtuosos
in the north and northeast parts. There are rare pheno-

98. pavan or allemande] pavin
or almain *Q 1–3.*

---

98. *pavan or allemande*] two grave and stately dances.

100. *benchers*] probably used here to mean one who officially sits on a
bench, a magistrate, judge, etc.; "a grave bencher." It might, however,
be meant to evoke the possibly grave movements of an inebriate; one who
frequents the benches of a tavern.

102–110. *Sir . . . thither.*] The Royal Society, through its secretary, kept
in constant touch with travelers to all parts of the world and sent by them
letters of inquiry about flora, fauna, customs, and so forth.

mena in those countries. I am beholden to Finland,
Lapland, and Russia for a great part of my philosophy.
I send my queries thither. —Come, Sir Formal, will you 110
help me to dispatch him?

SIR FORMAL.

I am proud to serve you.

SIR NICHOLAS [to Bruce *and* Longvil].

Be pleas'd to take a turn in the garden. When we have
dispatch'd, we will impart more of our microscopical
investigations.   115

BRUCE.

Your humble servant.   *Exeunt* Sir Formal *and* Sir Nicholas.
—This is a happy deliverance.

LONGVIL.

I have remov'd the lady by writing to Hazard to send for
her and keep her an·hour or two.

BRUCE.

And I have sent my man to find out Sir Nicholas his 120
strumpet. As soon as he has found her, she'll send for him.

LONGVIL.

For all his virtue and philosophy this grave fool will be in
the fashion too. Now if we can get rid of this wordy fool
Sir Formal, we have the ladies to ourselves. In the mean-
time, let's to our several and respective assignations.   125

                                        Exeunt.

[III.iv]   *Enter* Miranda *in the garden.*

MIRANDA.

What shall I say to this Bruce? O unjust custom that
has made women but passive in love as if nature had
intended us for ciphers only, to make up the number of
the creation.

                    Enter Bruce.

BRUCE.

Yonder's my Clarinda. Now love inspire me. —I am   5
infinitely transported with this honor you do me.

108. beholden] beholding *Q 1–3*.   [III.iv]
111. me] *Q 1; om. Q 2–3.*   0.1.] *scene division om. Q 1–3.*

MIRANDA.

If I have done you any honor, pray make your best on't.

BRUCE.

Is it you, madam? This honor was unexpected.

MIRANDA.

Why, whom did you expect? O, I see you are not so much
transported as you thought you were.   10

BRUCE.

The honor of your ladyship's company I did not expect.

MIRANDA.

Nor much care for, I see.

BRUCE.

'Twere blasphemy if I should say so. 'Twas your sister I
expected.

MIRANDA.

My sister! So, I am not fit for your company it seems.   15

BRUCE.

If I would tell you how I prize the honor, I should invade
the interest of my friend.

MIRANDA.

Your friend! If you had no more interest in .him than I
am resolv'd he shall ever have in me, he'd be the worst
friend you have.   20

BRUCE.

He's a man of honor and of wealth. And if any man could
deserve you, he might.

MIRANDA.

The world is not so barren but I have found a fitter man.
But, sir, 'twas not my sister, 'twas my Lady Gimcrack you
hop'd to meet here. You are a man of honor; the grotto is a   25
fine scene of love; the lady not very unwilling: 'twas well
you were interrupted, sir.

BRUCE [*aside*].

'Sdeath! How came she to know that? But I must bear it
out. —I cannot guess your meaning, but I see you love
your sister well to be jealous of her.   30

MIRANDA.

No, I assure you I have no reason to be jealous for her,
for to my knowledge she has irrecoverably dispos'd of her
heart in another place.

BRUCE [*aside*].

What's that? What says she? She's certainly jealous for
herself then. There must be something in this.   35

MIRANDA [*aside*].

In what confusion am I! This can never end well. —What.
I see you are troubled that I have told you a secret of my
sister's and discover'd one of yours. Come, walk and
consider on't.

BRUCE [*aside*].

I am surpris'd so I know not what to do in this exigence.   40

Exeunt.

Enter Longvil *and* Clarinda.

CLARINDA.

You stare about like a hare-finder. What's the matter?

LONGVIL.

Faith, madam, I expected to have met your sister here.

CLARINDA.

Say you so? The truth on't is she desired me to take the
trouble off her hands.

LONGVIL.

I am sorry, madam, she thinks it so.   45

CLARINDA.

You see, sir, I am content to suffer for her sake.

LONGVIL.

You have a mind to try me for your sister, madam.

CLARINDA.

No, I assure you, sir, she's resolved never to make trial of
you herself nor by another.

LONGVIL.

What can the meaning of this be?   50

CLARINDA.

Come, sir, I will be a little plainer with you. She has
dispos'd of her heart to another, without power of
revocation.

34. S.D. *aside*] *Q3; om. Q1–2.*   40. S.D. *aside*] *Q3; om. Q1–2.*
36. S.D. *aside*] *Q3; om. Q1–2.*

41. *hare-finder*] a man whose business it was to find or espy a hare. Cf.
Much Ado, I.i.186: "Or do you play the flouting Jack, to tell us Cupid is a
good hare-finder?"

LONGVIL.

Why would she not meet me to tell me so herself?

CLARINDA.

She thought me fitter for't. Besides, perhaps this has given 55
her an opportunity to see one she likes better.

LONGVIL.

I see, madam, she has not the same kindness for you, to
send you to one she likes so ill.

CLARINDA.

You do not know, but she may have taken as great a
trouble off my hands and kept me from one I like as ill as she 60
does you.

LONGVIL.

There's nothing but riddle in woman. They deceive as
much with the vizards of their mind as they do with those
of their faces.

CLARINDA.

I discover Sir Formal. We must be private no longer. 65

As they are going out enter Bruce *and* Miranda.

LONGVIL.

So Bruce, you are a happy man, I see.

BRUCE.

You are a pleasant one, I see. You and I must come to a
clearing of this business.

LONGVIL.

Ladies, we have something to impart to you, but shall be
hindered by this coxcomb Sir Formal. 70

CLARINDA.

We must have some consultations too with you. —Sister,
we'll catch him in a trap.

MIRANDA.

Here's a trapdoor of a vault where my uncle keeps his
bottles of air, which he weighs, of which you'll hear more
anon. We'll snap him in that, and then we shall have the 75
place to ourselves.

Enter Sir Formal.

CLARINDA.

Let me alone; I'll catch him.

SIR FORMAL.

Gentlemen and ladies, some affairs have engag'd my noble
friend Sir Nicholas to borrow himself of you awhile, and he
has commanded me to pawn my person till he shall redeem   80
it with his own.

MIRANDA.

Very quaintly express'd. We were just desiring your
company.

CLARINDA.

And we were admiring this talent of yours, your excellent
manner of speaking; and I've engag'd to give you a subject   85
to show your parts upon to these gentlemen.

SIR FORMAL.

Whatever is within the sphere of my activity, you must
command. I must confess I have some felicity in speaking.

MIRANDA.

Dear sister, give him a subject; you shall hear what oracles
hang on his lips. 'Tis all one what subject he speaks upon,   90
great or little.

SIR FORMAL.

That it is, madam. We orators speak alike upon all subjects.
My speeches are all so subtly design'd that whatever I speak
in praise of anything with very little alteration will serve
in praise of the contrary.   95

CLARINDA.

Let it be upon seeing a mouse enclosed in a trap.

SIR FORMAL.

'Tis all one to me; I am ready to speak upon all occasions.

CLARINDA.

Stand there, sir, while we place ourselves on each side.

SIR FORMAL.

I kiss your hand, madam. Now I am inspir'd with eloquence.
Hem. Hem. Being one day, most noble auditors, musing   100
in my study upon the too fleeting condition of poor human-
kind, I observed, not far from the scene of my meditation,
an excellent machine call'd a mousetrap (which my man
had plac'd there) which had included in it a solitary mouse,
which pensive prisoner, in vain bewailing its own mis-   105
fortunes and the precipitation of its too unadvised attempt,
still struggling for liberty against the too stubborn

opposition of solid wood and more obdurate wire; at last, the
pretty malefactor having tir'd alas, its too feeble limbs till
they became languid in fruitless endeavors for its excarcera- 110
tion, the pretty felon—since it could not break prison, and,
its offence being beyond the benefit of the clergy, could
hope for no bail—at last sat still, pensively lamenting the
severity of its fate and the narrowness of its, alas, too
withering durance. After I had contemplated awhile upon 115
the no little curiosity of the engine and the subtlety of its
inventor, I began to reflect upon the enticement which so
fatally betray'd the uncautious animal to its sudden ruin;
and found it to be the too, alas, specious bait of Cheshire
cheese, which seems to be a great delicate to the palate of 120
this animal, who, in seeking to preserve its life, O misfortune, took the certain means to death, and searching
for its livelihood had sadly encountered its own destruction.
Even so—

CLARINDA.

Now let the trap go.   125

SIR FORMAL.

Even so, I say—   *He sinks below.*

CLARINDA.

Even so, I say, have I catch'd the orator!

SIR FORMAL.

Help! Help! Murder!

LONGVIL.

Let the florid fool lie there.

MIRANDA.

I warrant him.   130

BRUCE.

He uses as many tropes and flourishes about a mousetrap as
he would in praise of Alexander.

Enter Sir Samuel *in woman's habit.*

SIR SAMUEL [*aside*].

This is the subtl'st disguise to make love in that e'er was

---

126. S.D. *He sinks below.*] Cf. *Mac Flecknoe*, ll. 211–215: ". . . but his last
words were scarcely heard,/ For Bruce and Longvil had a trap prepar'd,/
And down they sent the yet declaiming bard./ Sinking he left his drugget
robe behind,/ Borne upwards by a subterranean wind."

invented; this has serv'd me upon many intrigues. Well,
she shall see for all the sufferings of this day—to the tune of 135
kicking, beating, pumping, and tossing in a blanket, and
all that—that nothing shall hinder me in my love. Shall
Sir Samuel be frighted from an intrigue? No!

LONGVIL.

Whom have we here?

SIR SAMUEL.

Ladies, I was commanded by my Lady Pleasant to wait on 140
you with choice of good things, which she told me you
would buy.

MIRANDA.

What's the meaning of this?

CLARINDA.

Since she came from my lady we must see what she would
sell. 145

SIR SAMUEL.

I have choice of good gloves, amber, orangery, Genoa,
Roman, fragipande, neroli, tuberose, jessamine, and
marshal; all manner of tires for the head, locks, tours,
frowses, and so forth; all manner of washes, almond water,

---

136. and] *Q2–3;* and and *Q1.*   146. Genoa] *No comma follows in Q1.*

146–156. *I . . . tinderbox.*] Lloyd believes that in this scene Sir Samuel
speaks in the quasi-scientific jargon of Sir Kenelm Digby, when he offers
to sell Miranda and Clarinda beauty recipes, some, for example lamb's
caul, particularly associated with Digby's famous cures. Dryden certainly
had this scene and character in mind when he wrote in *Mac Flecknoe,* l. 181:
"Where sold he bargains, 'whip-stitch, kiss my arse."

146. *orangery*] a scent or perfume smelling of oranges.

146. *Genoa*] an Italian perfume from Genoa.

147. *Roman*] a perfume from Rome.

147. *fragipande*] perfume from or imitating the odor of the flower of the
red jasmine.

147. *neroli*] an oil distilled from the flowers of bitter oranges.

147. *tuberose, jessamine*] perfumes made from the tuberose and the jasmine.

148. *marshal*] according to Summers, the name of two popular French
perfumes.

148. *tires*] headdresses.

148. *locks*] a tress of artificial hair. (*OED* quotes this passage.)

148. *tours*] a crescent front of false hair.

149. *frowses*] a wig of frizzed hair. See I.ii.113.

and mercury water for the complexion; the best peter   150
and Spanish paper that ever came over; the best pomatums
of Europe, but one rare, one made of a lamb's caul and
May dew; also all manner of confections of mercury and
hog's bones to preserve present and to restore lost beauty.
If any outdoes me in these businesses, or have better goods   155
than I, I am the son of a tinderbox—[*Aside.*] O devil! What
did I say? I shall betray myself.

MIRANDA.

How's this, the son of a tinderbox?

SIR SAMUEL.

Pish, I mean the daughter of a tinderbox.

BRUCE [*aside*].

This is the rascal Sir Samuel in disguise.   160

SIR SAMUEL [*to* Miranda].

In the first place try a pair of gloves, madam. [*Whispers.*]
Don't you know me?

MIRANDA.

How should I know you?

SIR SAMUEL.

Let me tell you Sir Samuel's as true a lover as e'er wore a
head.   165

CLARINDA.

What's the meaning of this private discourse?

SIR SAMUEL [*aside*].

Pox on her envy! She's always for a cup of mischief. I'll put
this note into a glove, and that will do my business. Slapdash, as flat as a flounder. [*To* Clarinda.] I have no
private business. [*To* Miranda.] Be pleas'd to try on   170
this glove, madam. [*Whispers.*] Do not you know me
yet? I am Sir Samuel.

MIRANDA.

What's this, a note within it.

SIR SAMUEL [*to* Miranda].

Keep it to yourself.

---

150. *peter*] some kind of cosmetic, probably rouge, though it is also
associated with patches.

151. *Spanish paper*] cosmetic coming from or used in Spain, probably a
fine rouge.

152. *caul*] a free fold attached to the stomach and transverse colon; the
great ometum.

CLARINDA.

What note's that? From Sir Samuel Hearty? O Heav'n, 175
this is a bawd!

LONGVIL.

A downright bawd, and bawd to that rascal.

BRUCE.

'Sdeath! Pull the bawd in pieces.

MIRANDA.

Lay hold on the bawd. We'll have her carted. Seize her till
Sir Nicholas comes in. We'll have her sent to Bridewell and 180
soundly whipped there and then carted.

SIR SAMUEL [aside].

So! This is a fine, merry way of proceeding. I have made
nimble work on't. —Let me go; I am an honest woman
and labor in my vocation. Let me go; or as I am an honest
man, I'll sue you about this business. 185

LONGVIL.

How's this? A man! Nay then, I'll try a good kicking upon
you.

SIR SAMUEL.

Hold! Hold! What, do you mean to beat a woman? Will
you make me miscarry? I am with child, and for ought I
know, you have kill'd that within me. 190

BRUCE.

You said, "As you were an honest man."

SIR SAMUEL.

O dunce that I am! That's a way I have of expressing
myself. But I'll make you know I am a woman.

MIRANDA [to Clarinda].

It is my fool Sir Samuel. Prithee, Clarinda, let's put him
to Sir Formal and secure him till my uncle comes. It will 195
make excellent sport.

CLARINDA [to Miranda].

Do you set him upon the trap; it will do rarely.

MIRANDA [to Sir Samuel].

One word with you. Come this way, Sir Samuel. I cannot
tell you how much I am afflicted for your sufferings.

---

180. *Bridewell*] a London house of correction.
181. *carted*] carried in a cart as a punishment. Both Southerne (1692)
and Swift (1730) speak of "carted bawds."

SIR SAMUEL.

    'Shaw, it's no matter. Come, it's well it's no worse.   200

MIRANDA.

    Now Clarinda.   Sir Samuel *sinks*.

SIR SAMUEL.

    O murder, murder! Who's here? The devil?

CLARINDA.

    So now we have the garden to ourselves. Let's walk and
consult about our affairs.   *Exeunt*.

ACT IV

[IV.i]   Sir Formal *and* Sir Samuel *in the vault*.

SIR FORMAL [*aside*].

    I can no longer contain myself. This lady, join'd with
darkness and opportunity (the midwife of vice as we may so
say), has so inflam'd me that I must further attempt her
chastity. I am confident she must be handsome and no
mean person by her silken garments. —Madam, as I was   5
saying, since we are unwittingly enclos'd in darkness,
which yet cannot be so since enlightened by the rays of
your beauty—

SIR SAMUEL.

    For all your oratory about this business, I cannot see my
hand it is so dark.   10

SIR FORMAL.

    Ah, madam, the bright enlightener of the day by which
all creatures see is yet itself depriv'd of vision.

SIR SAMUEL [*aside*].

    Pox o' this damn'd rhetoric! What will become of me? I
must either discover myself (which I would not for the
world), or be sent to Bridewell and be whipped with a   15
certiorari. And yet methinks I have no need on't, for I have
been very plentifully kicked and beaten about this business
today already.

SIR FORMAL [*aside*].

    Let me be reveng'd on this fair enemy—the prettiest,
softest, and dissolving hand I ever had the honor to imprint   20

---

    16. *certiorari*] a writ, issuing from a superior court, upon the complaint
of a party that he has not received justice in an inferior court.

my kisses on. She has inflam'd me mightily. I'll try her
this way. —Do me the honor to accept of this purse and
the contents thereof.

SIR SAMUEL [aside].
I'll take the rogue's purse whate'er come on't.

SIR FORMAL.
Sweet lady, let's make our condition as happy as in us   25
lies.

SIR SAMUEL.
Nay, good sir, O Lord, sir! What do 'e mean? Fie, sir.

SIR FORMAL.
Let me approach the honor of your lip, far sweeter than
the phoenix nest and all the spicy treasures of Arabia.

SIR SAMUEL.
'Tis your goodness, sir, but pray forbear—   30

SIR FORMAL.
Nay, strive not; upon my sincerity I will.

SIR SAMUEL.
Nay, good sir, be not uncivil. I am no such person. Nay,
pish, I never saw the like. You are the strangest man. Well,
take it then. I vow you make me blush. [Aside.] If I
were not in apparent danger of being whipped damnably 35
and missing my masquerade, I could be merry with this
fool.

SIR FORMAL.
The sweets of Hybla dwell upon thy lips. Not all the
fragrant bosom of the spring affords such ravishing
perfumes.   40

SIR SAMUEL.
O Lord, sir, you are pleas'd to compliment. [Aside.] Ah
lying rogue, my breath smells of tobacco.

SIR FORMAL.
Our time may be but short; pardon the unbecoming rough-
ness which my passion prompts me to. Come, my dear
Cloris.   45

SIR SAMUEL.
Lord, what a pretty name is that. I was ne'er call'd Cloris
before.

---

38. *Hybla*] one of three towns of that name in Sicily; celebrated for its honey.
45. *Cloris*] a typically pastoral name; and the name of Sir Christopher's
whore in *The Woman Captive* (1680).

SIR FORMAL.

Come, my dear nymph, let us be more familiar. The
solitary darkness of the place invites us to love's silent
pleasures. Now, dearest Cloris, let us taste those sweets—   50

SIR SAMUEL.

Nay, pish, fie, Lord! What do you mean? What would you
be at? Keep off. I protest I'll call out. Nay, pish, never
stir I will.

SIR FORMAL.

Thou hast provok'd my gentle spirit so it has become
furious, and it is decreed I must enjoy thy lovely body—   55

SIR SAMUEL.

Out upon you! My body! I defy you. I am an honest
woman; I scorn your words. I will call out for somebody
to protect my honor.

SIR FORMAL.

Your honor cannot suffer. None can see us, and who will
declare it?   60

SIR SAMUEL.

Out upon you! Get you gone, you swine. I will not suffer
in my honor. I am virtuous. Help! Help! A rape! A rape!
Help! Help!

SIR FORMAL.

Be not obstreperous; none can hear you. You have provok'd me contrary to my gentle temper—even to a rape.   65
Come, I will, I must, i'faith I must.

SIR SAMUEL [aside].

'Sdeath! The rogue begins to pry into the difference of
sexes and will discover mine. I must try my strength with
him. —Out lustful Tarquin! You libidinous goat, have at
you.   70

        Sir Samuel *beats* Sir Formal, *kicks him, and flings him down.*

SIR FORMAL.

Help! Help! Murder! Murder!

SIR SAMUEL.

Be not obstreperous; none can hear you.

SIR FORMAL.

Upon my verity I think this be an Amazon! Well, I can
bear this, but—

SIR SAMUEL.

Do you again attempt my honor? I'll maul you, you   75
lascivious villain.

SIR FORMAL.

Hold, hold, I beseech you! I humbly rest contented. I
acquiesce.

SIR SAMUEL.

Get you from me, lustful swine. Be gone.

SIR FORMAL.

I go, madam. But I know not whether this vault doth   80
terminate here, or whether it doth issue further.   *They retire.*

[IV.ii]   *Scene: a bedchamber. Enter* Snarl *and* Mrs. Figgup.

SNARL.

Come, now we are safe in this hold none will interrupt us
in our great design. Ah pox o' these wicked hectors, vicious,
impudent rogues! A man cannot retire with a lady for his
private satisfaction but these ranting rogues must roar and
interrupt us. 'Tis a very impudent, vicious age, in sadness.   5

MRS. FIGGUP.

But my dear, if anybody else should have a key to this room
[*aside*] as I know they have though I dare not tell him— It
is a common scene of love matters.

SNARL.

Fear not; the landlady tells me nobody has a key but
myself. I have agreed to give her a guinea a week for these   10
private occasions. In sadness, 'tis a fine place. Here a man
may bring a lady, and even none of the house observe it.
There is not such a convenience in all the Pall Mall for
these occasions, though some there are much given to
such diversions. How glad am I to have thee here, poor   15
pig'snie—

MRS. FIGGUP.

Ah Lord! There's somebody at the door!

81. further] *Q1;* farther *Q2–3.*

---

2. *hectors*] braggarts, blusterers, bullies; applied specifically to a set of
disorderly young men who infested the streets of London in the second half
of the seventeenth century.

SNARL.

> In sadness, there is. There's one with a key too. In, into
> the woodhole quickly, or we shall be discover'd. Quick!
> Quick!   20

Enter Hazard *and* Lady Gimcrack.

HAZARD.

> Come, my dear lady, now we are safe from interruption.
> How happy am I in your favors.

LADY GIMCRACK.

> Ah, so you say; but if ever I hear of your inconstancy, you
> shall be no longer happy, as you call it. I cannot suffer a
> rival.   25

HAZARD.

> Nothing shall e'er divert me from the happiness I enjoy in
> you. Nor am I less impatient of a rival than you are. I am
> so covetous of you that the thought of your husband keeps
> me still inquiet.

LADY GIMCRACK.

> Fear not a husband. Husbands are such phlegmatic,   30
> indifferent rivals they ne'er can hurt the gallants; they,
> poor easy souls, do everything as if they did it not.

HAZARD.

> "They do but court and keep a pother
> To make one gamesome for another."

LADY GIMCRACK.

> You are in the right.   35

HAZARD.

> Nay, I think a husband is a very insipid, foolish animal and
> is growing mightily out of fashion.

LADY GIMCRACK.

> We shall begin to lay 'em by. Husbands will be left off as
> gentlemen-ushers are. Indeed they are more unnecessary
> instruments than those formal, spindle-shanked, finical fools   40
> with nosegays and white gloves were.

HAZARD.

> Those, though they could do no service themselves, would
> make way for them that could; but a husband is a clog, a

29. inquiet] *Q 1–2;* in quiet *Q 3.*   37. mightily] *Q 1; om. Q 2–3.*

dog in a manger, a miser that hoards up gold from others
and will not make use on't himself.   45

LADY GIMCRACK.

Nay, a thousand times worse. A miser would keep to himself
what he loves, and a husband what he does not care for.
Out on him. A husband's an insect, a drone, a dormouse—

HAZARD.

A foolish matrimonial lump—

LADY GIMCRACK.

A cuckoo in winter—   50

HAZARD.

An opiate for love—

LADY GIMCRACK.

A body without a soul—

HAZARD.

A chip in porridge—

LADY GIMCRACK.

A white of an egg—

HAZARD.

All phlegm and no choler—   55

LADY GIMCRACK.

A drudge—

HAZARD.

An excuse—

LADY GIMCRACK.

A necessary thing—

HAZARD.

A cloak at a pinch—

LADY GIMCRACK.

A pitiful utensil—   60

HAZARD.

Good for nothing but to cover shame, pay debts, and own
children for his wife.

LADY GIMCRACK.

In short, a husband is a husband, and there's an end of him.
But a lover is—

---

50. *A . . . winter*] the cuckoo appears in the spring.
53. *chip*] i.e., without flavor.
55. *All . . . choler*] sluggish, not irascible.

HAZARD.

>Not to be express'd but in action. I'll show you what a lover   65
>is with a vengeance, madam. Come on. —'Sdeath! There's
>a key in the door.

LADY GIMCRACK.

>What shall we do?

HAZARD.

>Run into the woodhole quickly. I'll bear the brunt, and I
>may perhaps make a discovery into the bargain. *She goes in.*   70

Enter Sir Nicholas *and* Mrs. Flirt.

SIR NICHOLAS.

>Come, dearest, the landlady is not at home, or we would
>have a collation here.

MRS. FLIRT.

>O Heav'n! Who's this! Hazard!

HAZARD.

>'Sdeath, sir! How dare you invade my room?

LADY GIMCRACK [*inside the woodhole*].

>O! Who's here? The devil! The devil!   75

Enter Lady Gimcrack.

>O Heav'n! Who's this! My husband with a whore!

SIR NICHOLAS.

>Death and hell! My wife with a hectorly fellow here! O my
>disgrace.

LADY GIMCRACK.

>O vile, false man! Thy falsehood I have long suspected.
>Now this happy opportunity has discover'd all.   80

SIR NICHOLAS.

>What means her impudence?

LADY GIMCRACK.

>Was I not sufficient for thee, vile man, but thou must thus
>betray me? I cannot look on thee with patience. I shall faint!
>I shall faint! O! O!

HAZARD.

>Help, help the lady.   85

SIR NICHOLAS.

>Hang the lady. O womankind, what artifice is this? I was
>inform'd by this lady I should find you here. I wonder not

at your disorder upon this unexpected surprise. O vile,
treacherous woman!

LADY GIMCRACK.

Take him from my sight; I shall die else. Have I been   90
always your obedient, virtuous wife and am I thus requited?
Heav'n sent this honorable gentleman to assist me in the
discovery, who on purpose got a key to this room—it seems
the filthy scene of all thy lust and baseness. Be gone, thou
infamous wretch; I am not able to support the sight of thee.   95

SIR NICHOLAS.

Lewd woman! Thou abstract of impudence and falsehood,
tremble at my revenge! Have I at length found out your
base, lascivious haunt?

LADY GIMCRACK.

O insufferable, do you add to all your barbarous injuries
this of aspersing my innocence?   100

MRS. FLIRT (*to* Hazard).

False man, did I for this give my affection to thee! And
canst thou think I'll bear this unreveng'd?

HAZARD (*aside*).

'Sdeath! This wench will undo me with my lady.

LADY GIMCRACK.

What do I hear? Is he false too? Then my misfortunes are
complete. (*To* Hazard.)   Base, vile, ungrateful fellow; is 105
this your constancy and gratitude to me?

HAZARD.

Madam, this is a lady of a great estate whom I should have
married, and this accident, I fear, has ruin'd all my fortune.

SIR NICHOLAS (*to* Mrs. Flirt).

Has my kindness deserv'd this? Is this your gallant too? O
this villain has made me doubly a cuckold.   110

MRS. FLIRT (*to* Sir Nicholas).

Do not mistake me. This fellow took me for a great fortune
and should have married me. (*To them.*)   Are you consult-
ing for my ruin?

LADY GIMCRACK (*to* Hazard).

This is a flam, I'll not believe it. This strumpet has doubly
betray'd me. Lewd creature, first I'll take revenge on thee. 115

---

114. *flam*] an act of deception.

MRS. FLIRT (*to* Lady Gimcrack).

>   I thought I should at last find out the cause of my mis-
>   fortune. (*To* Hazard.) You are like to make a good
>   husband that can make so ill a lover.

HAZARD.

>   After I have heard all your accusation, which is false, let
>   me tell you I have been informed of your frequent coming 120
>   hither with Sir Nicholas and was resolv'd at once to be
>   reveng'd of him and you by bringing my lady hither to
>   discover both.

MRS. FLIRT.

>   O insolence! I never saw the place before.

SIR NICHOLAS.

>   I am too well satisfied of her falsehood, and though it be 125
>   something below a philosopher to draw a sword, yet to
>   punish her I will.

HAZARD.

>   Hold, sir, first you must try with me.

SIR NICHOLAS.

>   What are you—her stallion and her bravo too?

LADY GIMCRACK.

>   Was ever woman yet so miserable? To be betray'd by one 130
>   whom she has lov'd so much better than her life! She
>   would have laid it down to have done him any kindness.
>   And yet to perfect all his cruelty he blots my reputation.
>   And since the only treasure of my life is gone, pray take
>   that too. —Do not resist him. Let him pierce this breast 135
>   that ne'er bore any image but his own. —Come on then,
>   cruel man.

SIR NICHOLAS.

>   What can this mean?

MRS. FLIRT (*to* Sir Nicholas).

>   For Heav'n's sake do not betray me to him. If I be not
>   clear'd in this I am undone.   140

HAZARD.

>   Now hear me, sir. This lady, on my honor, sir, is free from
>   all blemish, I believe even in thought. But I, being inform'd
>   you use to come with that lady to this house of ill reputation,
>   in anger to you both betray'd you to my lady. I dogg'd her
>   messenger from her lodging to you and immediately gave 145
>   notice to my lady. And in all haste we came—

SIR NICHOLAS.

Indeed I have been acquainted with this lady, being a
virtuosa, upon philosophical matters, but never saw her here
till we now came for this discovery. She inform'd me she
saw you two come hither, and my wife being gone out 150
before me and alone gave me more suspicion.

MRS. FLIRT.

I, having seen you privately talking with my lady in the
Mall, suspected you; and to revenge myself on her and you
I sent for him, and we have dogg'd you hither.

SIR NICHOLAS.

But why was she hidden to avoid my sight if she came for a 155
discovery?

HAZARD.

She thought to have discover'd more by being unseen and
overhearing your discourse.

LADY GIMCRACK.

Now see, injurious man, how you have wrong'd me.

SIR NICHOLAS (*to himself*).

Though I hope I have deceiv'd her with a lie, yet what she 160
says looks like truth.   (*To her.*)   It must be so. Come, no
more, I will believe you true, and so am I.

MRS. FLIRT [*to* Hazard].

Though this sham passes upon him, I know too well you
are guilty, good Mr. Hazard; and I hate you for't.

HAZARD [*to* Mrs. Flirt].

Prithee hold thy peace. I am kept by her as I know you 165
are by him. I am kept, I—

SIR NICHOLAS.

Heav'n knows I am true.

LADY GIMCRACK.

And Heav'n can witness for my innocence.

HAZARD.

I am glad that all things are thus happily clear'd.

SIR NICHOLAS.

But what was it frighted you within, my dear?   170

LADY GIMCRACK.

There is somebody in the woodhole.

HAZARD.

Now all's over I'll see who it is. —Come out here. What's
here? A woman—   *Pulls out* Mrs. Figgup.

LADY GIMCRACK.

A shame on her. How sneakingly she looks! This is some
strumpet I warrant you. O, foh, how I hate such cattle! 175
[*Aside*.]   Heav'n grant she did not hear me and Hazard.

HAZARD.

Here's a man too. —Come out of your hole. Mr. Snarl, is it
you!   *Pulls him out by the heels.*

SIR NICHOLAS.

Is this the fruit of your virtue and declaiming against the
vice of the age!   180

LADY GIMCRACK [*aside*].

Heav'n! If he overheard me I am ruin'd eternally. I'll try
him. —We met all here upon a mistake which is now
happily rectified. But 'tis too apparent, uncle, you came for
wickedness and abomination.

MRS. FIGGUP.

I scorn your words, madam. I am civil and virtuous.   185

SNARL.

Ay, in sadness, are we. Our intentions were honorable. I
met this lady upon a virtuous account, by the mass. I love
and honor her in a civil way and scorn your filthy, lascivious
beasts of this age.

SIR NICHOLAS.

Remember, sir, I have you on the hip. No more will I 190
endure your frumps and taunts about my philosophy and the
noble exercise of my parts.

SNARL.

Nephew, let me tell you, you are an ass, in sadness; and I
will make you know this lady is virtuous, yes, as virtuous as
your ladyship. And I will defend her honor with my sword, 195
by the mass; and he that dares be so presumptuous to
contradict it, let him draw.

He draws.

SIR NICHOLAS.

Gad forgive me, what means he?

HAZARD.

No, none are so much concern'd at it— But what are these
rods which I drew out with you? What do they mean?   200

180. vice] *Q 1–2;* vices *Q 3.*

SNARL [*aside*].

O devil, I shall be betray'd. —Ha! Rods! What a pox know
I what they are? I believe the mistress of the house is a school
mistress.

HAZARD.

Yes, she keeps a very virtuous school for the disciplining
of hopeful, towardly old gentlemen.   205

MRS. FIGGUP.

Now my honor's clear. Let's go, sir. Besides, here's that
base creature Flirt. I cannot abide the sight of her since
she discommended thee, my dear.

SNARL.

Come, madam. In sadness, this is very fine. Two civil
persons cannot meet privately in an affectionate way but 210
such as you must censure them. But I will make you know
this lady is honorable. I will, in sadness. And so fare you well.

Exeunt Snarl *and* Mrs. Figgup.

SIR NICHOLAS.

Come, my dear, now let's go home. Do not grieve at my
unhappy jealousy since my belief of thy dear truth is more
confirm'd by it. Come, my dear.   215

Exeunt.

[IV.iii]

Enter Longvil, Bruce, Miranda, *and* Clarinda [*and* Maid].

MIRANDA.

Come, to divert this insipid talk of love (a theme so threadbare no man can speak new sense upon it), my maid shall
sing you a new song she learned the other day.

CLARINDA.

You must not expect much wit in it, for poets are grown
such good husbands they'll lay out none upon a song.   5

MIRANDA.

All we must look for is smooth verse and a good tune.

CLARINDA.

And how a good tune and tinkling rhyme atones for nonsense, the songsters and heroics of the time may sufficiently
convince you.

201. S.D. *aside*] *Q3; om. Q1–2.*   [IV.iii]
                                     4. not] *Q1, 3; om. Q2.*

MIRANDA.

They make nonsense go down as glib without tasting as a   10
seditious lie is swallow'd in a city coffeehouse or commonwealth club—without examination.

CLARINDA.

But now let's hear it.

[MAID *sings*.]

       "How wretched is the slave to love,
       Who can no real pleasures prove,   15
       For still they're mixed with pain.
       When not obtain'd, restless is the desire.
       Enjoyment puts out all the fire
       And shows the love was vain.

       "It wanders to another soon,   20
       Wanes and increases like the moon,
       And like her never rests;
       Brings tides of pleasure now, and then of tears;
       Makes ebbs and flows of joys and cares
       In lovers' wavering breasts.   25

       "But spite of love I will be free,
       And triumph in the liberty
       I without him enjoy.
       I' th' worst of prisons I'll my body bind
       Rather than chain my freeborn mind   30
       For such a foolish toy."   [Maid *exits*.]

LONGVIL.

'Tis very well, madam.

BRUCE.

But to us there is no music like love, or harmony like the
consent of lovers' hearts.

MIRANDA.

But as music is improv'd by practice, love decays by it, and   35
therefore I scarce dare talk on't.

CLARINDA.

Let what harmony soever be between lovers at first, in a

14–31. "*How wretched . . . foolish toy.*"] Music ascribed to Francis
Forcer; published in *Choice Ayres and Songs to Sing to the Theorbo-Lute or Bass-
Viol . . . The Second Book . . .* London, Printed by Anne Godbid, and are
Sold by John Playford . . . 1679. P. 6.

37–43. *Let . . . jangle.*] Cf. Horace, "concordia discors," *Epis.* I.xii.19;
Hamlet, III.i.56, "Like sweet bells jangled out of tune and harsh."

short time it turns to scurvy jangling. And therefore can you
blame us if we divert so dangerous a thing any way?

LONGVIL.

I confess it may come to discord, but 'tis as in music: if it be   40
good, it makes the following concord better.

BRUCE.

If they play upon one another till they are out of tune, they
must needs jangle.

LONGVIL.

In that case they must lay by and tune again and then
strike up afresh.   45

MIRANDA.

That simile will never hold. For when love grows once out
of tune, they may screw and keep a coil, but 'twill never
stand in tune again.

CLARINDA.

'Tis most certain: when love comes once to bend, it breaks
presently.   50

BRUCE.

But perhaps it may be set again like a broken limb and be
the stronger for't.

MIRANDA.

No. When love breaks, 'tis into so many splinters; 'tis never
to be set again.

Enter Maid *to* Miranda.

MAID.

Shift for yourselves; Sir Nicholas and my lady are both   55
return'd home again.

CLARINDA.

O mischievous ill fortune.

MIRANDA.

Unlucky accident.

CLARINDA.

I must look after Sir Formal.   *Exeunt Ladies.*

LONGVIL.

Their carriage since their cross appointment in the garden   60
has too evidently declar'd their intentions. We have mistaken I see. If we design to succeed, we must change
mistresses.

BRUCE.

> 'Tis too evident we have plac'd our loves wrong. They are
> both handsome, rich, and honest—three qualities that   65
> seldom meet in women.

LONGVIL.

> 'Tis true. And since 'twill be necessary after all our rambles
> to fix our unsettled lives to be grave, formal, very wise, and
> serve our country, and propagate our species, let us think
> on't here.   70

BRUCE.

> Let us walk and consult about this weighty affair.
>
> *Exeunt* Bruce *and* Longvil.

> *Enter* Sir Nicholas, Lady Gimcrack, Clarinda, Miranda.

SIR NICHOLAS.

> A woman with a letter, a tire woman too! Are they all
> bawds? Their very art of washing and adorning women is
> implicit bawding, but this is downright explicit bawdry.

MIRANDA.

> Good sir, let her be made an example to all vile women.   75

CLARINDA.

> We have secur'd her in the vault here.

SIR NICHOLAS.

> You have done well. She shall be brought to condign
> punishment.

MIRANDA.

> But we can tell you yet a stranger thing: Sir Formal is
> privately shut up with this lewd woman, and has been this   80
> hour.

CLARINDA.

> 'Tis very true. What his intentions are I know not, but 'tis a
> very scandalous thing.

SIR NICHOLAS.

> *O monstrum horrendum!* Is my friend, that seeming virtuous
> man, fall'n into the snare?   85

65. both] *Q1, 3; om. Q2.*

---

77. *condign*] appropriate.

84. *O monstrum horrendum*] "O fearful monster," Virgil, *Aeneid*, III.658;
said of the one-eyed giant, Polyphemus.

LADY GIMCRACK.

O virtue, whither art thou fled? My house is dishonored,
abus'd. I am ready to faint when I hear of lewdness. My
dear, do not endure it. I shall never endure my house
again. Let it with all speed, and let's remove.

SIR NICHOLAS.

Prithee, dear, be pacified.   90

LADY GIMCRACK.

O I cannot be pacified. My blood rises when I hear of lewd,
whoring fellows. I would have 'em all hang'd.

MIRANDA [aside].

Excellent hypocrite!

SIR NICHOLAS.

Well, Heav'n be prais'd, I am the happiest man in a wife.
I will rebuke him, but for the bawd I'll have a warrant   95
from the next justice. I will have her whipped and carted.
Come, bring 'em out here.

       Servants bring in Sir Formal *and* Sir Samuel.

—Truly Sir Formal, I am much asham'd to find a virtuoso
in such a posture with a lewd woman.

SIR FORMAL.

Why, sir, upon my sincerity.   100

LADY GIMCRACK.

Out upon you. Have you the face to speak in your own
defence or in defence of this odious vice? Out on't! You
think to bring all off with your eloquence, but I'll not hear
it. You have defil'd my house and committed lewdness
within the walls.   105

SIR FORMAL.

Why, ladies, you know—

MIRANDA.

What, you are angry we have discover'd you.

CLARINDA.

Would you have had us keep your pernicious counsel? Had
that been becoming our virtue?

SIR FORMAL.

Why, Sir Nicholas, I profess—   110

LADY GIMCRACK.

I cannot suffer it. 'Tis fit such hypocrites should be punish'd.

Is this your virtue, your sereneness of mind? And are all
your flowers of rhetoric come to this?

SIR NICHOLAS.

I know not what to say in your excuse. To retire with such
a lewd creature: I did not think you could have fall'n into 115
so shameful a scandal. I am sorry, since 'twill be a reproach
to all virtuosos.

SIR FORMAL.

By my integrity.

LADY GIMCRACK.

You are a man of integrity—to meet privately with a
filthy creature, a bawd, an ugly bawd too! 120

SIR SAMUEL.

I scorn your words; neither a bawd nor ugly, neither, by
your leave. —Ugly and bawd, quoth she!

SIR FORMAL.

Can I not be heard? Shall oratory have no place?

LADY GIMCRACK.

You think to bewitch us with your oratory, but 'tis too
apparent. You have dishonor'd my house. 125

SIR FORMAL.

Here are some phenomena of scandal, but I will dissolve all
in a punctum of time.

> Lady Gimcrack *and* Sir Formal *both speak at the same time.*

LADY GIMCRACK.

I will never endure you. You shall solve none of your
phenomena here more.

SIR FORMAL.

'Tis true, I confess I was found here privately with this 130
woman, but no less true—

SIR NICHOLAS [*to* Lady Gimcrack].

Pray let me hear him speak.

SIR FORMAL.

My oratory was never slighted before. When did I open
my mouth in vain before? I confess—

MIRANDA.

Why look you, sir, he confesses it. What would you have? 135

113. come] *Q 1–2; om. Q 3.*   127.1. at . . . time] *together Q 1–3.*

---

127. *a punctum of time*] an instant.

CLARINDA.

　　Will you not believe us he has been privately with her this
　　hour?

SIR NICHOLAS.

　　I say, peace. I will hear him.

SIR FORMAL.

　　I confess to you all—

MIRANDA.

　　D'you see again he confesses to us all—   140

Enter Snarl.

SIR FORMAL.

　　Now my shame comes upon me.

SNARL.

　　What, is my florid fool catch'd with a whore? An ugly
　　whore? Does your noble soul operate clearly without the
　　clog of your sordid, human body now? You are a fine,
　　formal hypocrite, in sadness. By the mass, it's a fine world 145
　　we live in.

SIR NICHOLAS.

　　I am confident my friend is innocent.

SIR SAMUEL.

　　He innocent! Hang him, he would have ravish'd me if I
　　had not been stronger than he and beaten him soundly.
　　My honor had suffer'd upon that business—   150

SIR FORMAL.

　　O tempora! O mores! But I doubt not but I shall shine clearer
　　after this eclipse. I will bear these wrongs with a serene
　　temper of mind.

SNARL.

　　Hang you, never trust your orator. In sadness, they will all
　　lie like dogs. By the mass, I would go fifty miles to see an 155
　　orator hang'd. Orators are rogues, the very grievances of
　　the nation, always putting in an oar, and prating and
　　disturbing the business of the nation with their foolish tropes,
　　and care not which way matters go so they may show their
　　parts.   160

---

　　151. *O tempora! O mores!*] "O, what an age, O what morals!" Cicero,
First Oration against Catiline, I.i.2.

SIR NICHOLAS.

    I do believe you, Sir Formal. —You young sluts, will you
never leave?

MIRANDA.

    Will you not take the woman's word?

SIR NICHOLAS.

    What, a bawd's word! She suffer in her honor, one that
brought a letter to you!   165

SIR SAMUEL.

    A bawd! I scorn your words. I brought a letter from a
gentleman that makes honorable love and would marry her.

SNARL.

    A matchmaker! That's worst of all.

SIR NICHOLAS.

    Your marriage bawd, your canonical bawd, is worst of all;
they betray people for their lifetimes. —Here, carry her and 170
lock her up in the green room. —I'll maul your bawdship.

SIR SAMUEL [*aside*].

    O Heav'n! I shall be whipped, nay, which is ten times
worse, I shall disappoint the town and have no masquerade
tonight. But I'll bail myself with money if it be possible.

MIRANDA [*to Sir Samuel*].

    Courage. My sister brought this upon you, but I'll redeem 175
all.

SIR SAMUEL [*aside*].

    Nay, if I succeed in my love, I care not if I be beaten,
kicked, and whipped—as if Heav'n and earth would come
together.

LADY GIMCRACK.

    Come, I'll see her locked up safe myself, filthy creature.   180

                    Exit Lady Gimcrack [*with* Sir Samuel].

CLARINDA [*to* Sir Formal].

    Not a word more o' this business. I could not forbear the
trick, but you will find me more favorable.

SIR FORMAL [*to* Clarinda].

    I shall be content to suffer anything for your sweet sake.

                    Exeunt Clarinda *and* Miranda.

            Enter Longvil *and* Bruce.

177–178. beaten, kicked] *Q1–2;*   *Q1–2.*
beaten, and kicked *Q3.*   181. S.D. *to* Sir Formal] *Q3; om.*
180.1. *with* Sir Samuel] *Q3; om.*   *Q1–2.*

SNARL.

> If you had come sooner you might ha' taken this orator,
> this flashy fellow, with a whore, in sadness, a foul, deform'd   185
> strumpet.

SIR FORMAL.

> Upon my honor, gentlemen, I am wrong'd; but he was
> taken with a lady and rods, too, in German Street, about
> an hour since.

LONGVIL.

> What, this virtuous gentleman of the last age!   190

BRUCE.

> One that so justly reproaches the vices of this! It cannot be.

SNARL.

> O dog! Rogue! Nephew, I'll be reveng'd. No, it cannot be,
> it is not. The orator's a son of a whore, and my nephew a
> foolish, rascally philosopher: one good for nothing but an
> empty noise of florid words without sense, in sadness; and   195
> the other good for nothing but useless experiments upon flies,
> maggots, eels in vinegar, and the blue upon plums, which
> he finds to be living creatures. But all the world will find
> him an ass, and so I leave him and all of ye, with a pox t'
> ye. —But in sadness, orator, I will beat thee mightily. I   200
> with a whore! I scorn your words, by the mass.

> > > > > > > > > > > > > > > > > > > *Exit* Snarl.

SIR NICHOLAS.

> I know he is in a rage, but 'tis true. Sir Formal, we'll no
> more endure his taunts. —But now he talks of eels, I'll show
> you millions in a saucer of vinegar. They resemble other
> eels save in their motion, which in others is sideways, but   205
> in them upwards and downwards thus, and very slow.

LONGVIL.

> We have heard of these, sir, often.

SIR NICHOLAS.

> Another difference is these have sharp stings in their tails.
> By the way, the sharpest vinegar is most full of 'em.

202. he is] *Q 1, 3;* he's *Q 2.*

---

188 *German Street*] now spelled Jermyn, a street between Piccadilly and
Pall Mall in the new and fashionable section of London around St. James'
Square.

BRUCE.

Then certainly the sharpness or biting of vinegar proceeds 210
from those stings striking upon the tongue.

SIR NICHOLAS.

I see you are a most admirable observer. It must needs be
so. [*Aside.*]   So, this is a rare phenomenon solv'd by the
by. —I have often concluded that before. The whole air is
full of living creatures a thousand times less visible than 215
those living creatures mistaken for motes in the sun. I know
most of 'em distinctly by my glasses.

SIR FORMAL.

Talk of use! These are the mysteries of nature's closet.

BRUCE [*aside*].

This foolish virtuoso does not consider that one bricklayer
is worth forty philosophers.   220

SIR NICHOLAS.

Then for the blue upon plums, it is nothing but many
living creatures. I have observ'd upon a wall plum (with
my most exquisite glasses, which cost me several thousands
of pounds) at first beginning to turn blue, it comes first to
fluidity, then to orbiculation, then fixation, so to anguliza- 225
tion, then crystallization, from thence to germination or
ebullition, then vegetation, then plantanimation, perfect
animation, sensation, local motion, and the like.

Enter Servant *to* Sir Nicholas.

SERVANT.

Sir, there are a great number of sick men waiting in the hall

227. plantanimation] *Q3;* plant-
ananimation *Q1–2.*

221–228. *Then . . . like.*] As Lloyd has pointed out, the whole passage is
taken from Robert Hooke's *Micrographia*, p. 127, in a passage describing
blue mould. The order of the scientific words is identical except that
Hooke concludes with "imagination," not "local motion."
   225. *orbiculation*] the formation or rounding of an orb or sphere. (*OED*
quotes this passage.)
   225–226. *angulization*] angular or cornered formation. (*OED* quotes only
this use of the word; Hooke had used it in 1665.)
   227. *ebullition*] act, process, or state of boiling or bubbling up.
   227. *plantanimation*] a plant-like animal growth; a zoophyte or "plant-
animal."

for your worship, and desire to be dispatch'd.   *Exit.* 230

SIR NICHOLAS.

Now, gentlemen, you shall see my method of practice. —Sir
Formal, will you go and rank 'em?

SIR FORMAL.

I obey in my wonted office. —Gentlemen, I humbly kiss
your hands.   *Exit.*

SIR NICHOLAS.

He ranks the diseas'd people in their several classes, forms, 235
or orders of diseases. To save trouble, you shall see all.

Servant *returns.*

SERVANT.

Sir, the constable is come with a warrant to carry the bawd
away.   [*Exit.*]

SIR NICHOLAS.

Come, we will deliver the bawd into their clutches, and
when I have administered to my sick, we'll take the air. By 240
the way, gentlemen, what country air do you like best?

BRUCE.

Why we cannot travel far for't this evening.

SIR NICHOLAS.

Travel! I thought I should have you. Why I never travel; I
take it in a close chamber.

LONGVIL.

Why you can take but one kind of nasty, smoky air in a 245
chamber.

SIR NICHOLAS.

There's your mistake. Choose your air, you shall have it in
my chamber: Newmarket, Banstead Down, Wiltshire, Bury
air, Norwich air; what you will.

BRUCE [*to* Longvil].

Would a man think it possible for a virtuoso to arrive at 250
this extravagance?

LONGVIL [*to* Bruce].

Yes, I assure you. It is beyond the wit of man to invent such
extravagant things for them as their folly finds out for

236.1. Servant *returns*] *Q1–2; Re-*   250. *think*] *Q1–2; thing Q3.*
enter Servant *Q3.*

-103-

themselves. —Is it possible to take all these several country
airs in your chamber?   255

SIR NICHOLAS.

I knew you were to seek. I employ men all over England,
factors for air, who bottle up air and weigh it in all places,
sealing the bottles hermetically. They send me loads from all
places. That vault is full of country air.

BRUCE.

To weigh air and send it to you!   260

SIR NICHOLAS.

O yes, I have sent one to weigh air at the peak of Teneriffe;
that's the lightest air. I shall have a considerable cargo of
that air. Sheerness and the Isle of Dogs' air is the heaviest.
Now if I have a mind to take country air, I send for maybe
forty gallons of Bury air, shut all my windows and doors   265
close, and let it fly in my chamber.

BRUCE.

This is a most admirable invention.

LONGVIL.

But to what purpose do you weigh air?

SIR NICHOLAS.

That I shall tell you as we are taking it. Now let's see this
bawd dispos'd of. Everything in its order.   *Exeunt.* 270

[IV.iv]   Sir Samuel *in the chamber solus.*

SIR SAMUEL.

How long shall I expect my fate? Well, there never was
such a martyr in love—to be kicked, beaten, pump'd, toss'd
in a blanket about business, and now in danger of being
whipped with a slapdash. But she loves me! Come, 'tis well
'tis no worse. But to miss my masquerade, that's the sum of 5

0.1.] *scene division om.* Q 1–3.   0.1. *solus*] Q 1–2; alone Q 3.

256–266. *I knew . . . chamber.*] See Introduction, pp. xxi–xxii.
261. *peak of Teneriffe*] rises about 12,200 feet in the Canary Islands.
263. *Sheerness*] on the Isle of Sheppey, North Kent, on the Thames
estuary at the mouth of the Medway.
263. *Isle of Dogs'*] a district of London in a bend of the Thames opposite
Greenwich.

all. But I'll bribe my justice and escape. 'Tis a trade; some
of the justices are liker malefactors than magistrates. But
'twill cost me a plaguy deal, for this damn'd virtuoso will
prosecute furiously. Ha, what's here, a rope! I am deliver'd
as Rabby Busie was by miracle. I'll slide down from the   10
window into the garden. The back door's open. So I save
my money *ipso facto* and go to my ball, and whipstitch,
your nose in my breech, Sir Nicholas. I'll leave my clothes
behind me. Though I am bawd above, I am Sir Samuel
underneath. So tire woman, lie thou there, and away knight.   15
'Tis well 'tis no worse.   *Exit.*

Enter Sir Nicholas, Longvil, Bruce, Lady Gimcrack, Clarinda,
Miranda, *Servants, Constable, Officers.*

SIR NICHOLAS.

Come, where is this bawd? Now we shall make her an
example. Here! Where are you? Ha, here's nobody.

LADY GIMCRACK.

I am sure I saw her locked in.

SERVANT.

The door was locked when we came in. Here are her clothes   20
too.

LONGVIL.

The rogue has stripped himself and has escap'd naked.

LADY GIMCRACK.

O Heav'n, this must be the devil. The house is haunted.

Enter Sir Formal.

SIR FORMAL.

I have set all the sick men in order, and they wait for your
prescription.   25

MIRANDA.

O Sir Formal, your mistress is flown and has left her case
behind her.

---

10. *Rabby Busie*] Zeal-of-the-Land Busy in Ben Jonson's *Bartholomew
Fair* is called Rabbi Busy (ed. Edward B. Partridge, IV.iv. 77); and when
through the actions of a madman he escapes the stocks, he says: "We are
delivered by miracle . . ." (V.i.156).

LADY GIMCRACK.

> The doors are fast, and she is flown out of the chimney. Have a care, Sir Formal, if you were naught with her, you will be torn in pieces. 30

SIR FORMAL.

> Not I, upon my sincerity.

SIR NICHOLAS.

> It was undoubtedly a spirit. I could have told you that before, but I was afraid I should fright you all.

BRUCE.

> How, sir! Was it a spirit say you?

SIR NICHOLAS.

> You must know, sir, I am much skill'd in Rosicrucian 35 learning. I am one of the *vere adepti* as simple as I stand here. I discover'd it by my sight having familiar conversation with spirits.

CLARINDA [*aside*].

> O the subtlety of this virtuoso! This notable spirit Sir Samuel makes a ball tonight. We will steal out one way or 40 other.

BRUCE.

> You'll remember the masquerade, ladies.

MIRANDA.

> Yes, yes, we will see the spirit.

LADY GIMCRACK [*aside*].

> I see your cross love and will plague ye, ye young sluts, for it. 45

SIR NICHOLAS.

> You converse with a great many people which you take to be men and women, but we Rosicrucians know 'em to be spirits. Now let us go to my sick people and administer.

> > *Exeunt.*

---

29. *naught*] (now obsolete) immoral, naughty (*OED* B.2).

32–38. *It was . . . spirits.*] Lloyd considers this passage on spirits and Rosicrucianism a satiric reference to Henry More and Joseph Glanvill, who had defended belief in the existence of spirits and witches.

36. *vere adepti*] one completely skilled in the secrets of his art; used by alchemists who professed to have attained the great secret. Cf. Butler, *Hudibras*, I.i.545–546: "In Rosicrucian lore as learned/ As he that *vere adeptus* earned."

[IV.v]

Scene is the courtyard full of several Lame and Sick People. Enter Sir Nicholas,
Sir Formal, Longvil, *and* Bruce [*and* Servant].

SICK PEOPLE.

    Heav'n bless your worship.

SIR NICHOLAS.

    Come, gentlemen, you must know I have studied all manner
    of cases and have bills ready written for all diseases. That's
    my way; I give 'em advice for nothing.

SIR FORMAL.

    Not more resorted to the temple of Aesculapius; I am sure   5
    not so many found relief as from my noble friend. —You
    have reason, good languishing people, to be trumpeters to
    his illustrious fame, whose indefatigable care for the good
    of feeble and distress'd mankind with his transcendent skill
    each day cures even incurable diseases.   10

LONGVIL [*aside*].

    Your orators are very subject to that figure in speech call'd
    a bull.

SIR NICHOLAS.

    I still administer'd to the incurable in Italy and never fail'd
    of success. Here are my bills. Where is the roll? Call it over.

SIR FORMAL.

    Gout.   15

TWO [WITH] GOUT (*halting*).

    Here.

SIR NICHOLAS.

    There's a bill for you two. Take it betwixt you.

SIR FORMAL.

    Stone.

TWO [WITH] STONES.

    Here, sir.

SIR NICHOLAS.

    There's one for you two.   20

SIR FORMAL.

    Scurvy.

---

  3. *bills*] prescriptions. Cf. l. 14 below.
 12. *bull*] a ludicrous jest or self-contradictory proposition.

FOUR [WITH] SCURVY.
>   Here, sir.

SIR NICHOLAS.
>   There's a bill for you four.

SERVANT.
>   Go, pass by as you are serv'd.

SIR FORMAL.
>   Consumption.   25

A CONSUMPTIVE.
>   Here.

SIR NICHOLAS.
>   Take your bill.

SIR FORMAL.
>   Dropsy.

TWO [WITH] DROPSY.
>   Here, sir.

SIR NICHOLAS.
>   There's for you two.   30

SIR FORMAL.
>   There is a madman I have set by for transfusion of blood.

SIR NICHOLAS.
>   That's well. The truth on't is we shall never get any but
>   madmen for that operation. But proceed.

SIR FORMAL.
>   These are the last but not the least. Pox.

Enter a great number of men and women.

ALL.
>   Here, here, here.   35

SIR NICHOLAS.
>   There are three or four bills for you, you are so many.

ALL.
>   Heav'n bless your worship.   *Exeunt omnes.*

ACT V

[V.i]   *Enter* Sir Formal *and* Clarinda.

SIR FORMAL.
>   How long shall I languish in expectation of your noble

favor, for the enjoyment of which my desires are as great
as my deserts are little.

CLARINDA.

Truly, Sir Formal, I am so sensible of your service and so
troubled with my confinement under my uncle that at   5
length I have determin'd by you to free myself from him.

SIR FORMAL.

Hold, madam, I am too suddenly blessed. I am all rapture,
all ecstasy. My soul, methinks, is fled from its corporeal
clog, and I am all unbodied, divinest lady. Let me kneel
and adore that hand, that snowy hand, to which the snow   10
itself is tann'd and sunburnt.

CLARINDA.

Not too much of this. But in short, conduct my sister and
me out of these doors to the masquerade, for we cannot
get out without your authority with the porter. And after
you have return'd to my uncle sometime, procure the habit   15
of Scaramouche that I may know you, and come to us, and
you shall absolutely dispose of me.

SIR FORMAL.

Madam, I'll fly, nay, outfly Sir Nicholas himself to do you
service, or any virtuoso in England. But how shall I know
you? You'll be disguis'd.   20

CLARINDA.

I'll find you out. Besides, you know this ring and bracelet.
We must have our maids with us, for we'll not return.
Let's find my sister and about it instantly.

SIR FORMAL.

I am all obedience. I should not envy now an universal
monarch. I hear my lady's voice.   *Exeunt.*   25

12. sister] sisters *Q 1–3.*   16. Scaramouche] Scaramoncha
                                           Q 1–3.

---

16. *Scaramouche*] a stock character in Italian farce, a cowardly and
foolish boaster of his own prowess who is constantly being cudgeled by
Harlequin. Scaramouche's costume, intended in ridicule of the Spanish don,
was usually black and was often adopted in masquerades. The clever
impersonation of the part by Tiberio Fiurelli, who brought his troop to
London in 1673, rendered the word very popular in England in the last
quarter of the seventeenth century.

[V.ii]

Enter Sir Nicholas, Longvil, *and* Servant *to Sir Nicholas.*

SERVANT.

    Mr. Bruce is coming to wait on you.   [*Exit.*]

Enter Bruce.

SIR NICHOLAS.

    Sir, your servant. [*To* Servant.] Now open the bottles
and let the air fly. —Gentlemen, be ready to snuff it up. O
this Bury air is delicate, 'tis delicious. O very refreshing.

BRUCE.

    O admirable. Who would go to Bury to take it?   5

SIR NICHOLAS.

    Not I, 'tis much the better here. It takes so much the
fresher for being bottled, as other liquors do. For let me tell
you, gentlemen, air is but a thinner sort of liquor and
drinks much the better for being bottled.

LONGVIL.

    Most certainly the world is very foolish not to snuff up   10
bottled air as they drink bottled drink.

BRUCE.

    The foolish world is never to be mended. For all this, your
glass coach will to Hyde Park for air. The suburb fools
trudge to Lamb's Conduit or Tottenham. Your sprucer sort
of citizen gallop to Epsom. Your mechanic, gross fellows,   15
showing much conjugal affection, strut before their wives,
each with a child in his arms, to Islington or Hogsdon.

SIR NICHOLAS.

    Ay, poor, dull fools.

LONGVIL.

    But to what end do you weigh this air, sir?

SIR NICHOLAS.

    To what end should I—to know what it weighs. O knowl-   20
edge is a fine thing. Why I can tell to a grain what a gallon
of any air in England weighs.

0.1.] *scene division om. Q 1–3. This   chamber (see IV.iii.244, 255, 266).*
scene takes place in Sir Nicholas'

---

   8. *air . . . liquor*] See Introduction, p. xxi.
   15. *mechanic*] low, vulgar.

BRUCE.

Is that all the use you make of these pneumatic engines?

SIR NICHOLAS.

No, I eclipse the light of rotten wood, stinking whitings and
thornback, and putrid flesh, when it becomes lucid.   25

LONGVIL.

Will stinking flesh give light like rotten wood?

SIR NICHOLAS.

O yes. There was a lucid sirloin of beef in the Strand.
Foolish people thought it burned when it only became
lucid and crystalline by the coagulation of the aqueous
juice of the beef by the corruption that invaded it. 'Tis   30
frequent. I myself have read a Geneva Bible by a leg of
pork.

BRUCE.

How, a Geneva Bible by a leg of pork!

SIR NICHOLAS.

O ay, 'tis the finest light in the world. But for all that, I
could eclipse the leg of pork in my receiver by pumping   35
out the air. But immediately upon the appulse of the air
let in again, it becomes lucid as before.

LONGVIL.

Is it so curious a light?

SIR NICHOLAS.

O admirable. I am now studying of glowworms, a fine study;
it is a curious animal. I think I shall preserve 'em light all   40
the year, and then I'll never use any other light in my study
but glowworms and concave glasses.

BRUCE.

What do you with the speaking trumpet?

SIR NICHOLAS.

O, that stentrophonical tube, though not invented by me,
yet is improv'd beyond all men's expectations.   45

24–37. *the light . . . before.*] On the "light of rotten wood" and the
"lucid sirloin" see Introduction, p. xxii.

44. *stentrophonical tube*] On April 2, 1668, Pepys described the "Otacous-
ticon" he examined at the Royal Society, "which was only a great glass
bottle, broke at the bottom, putting the neck to my eare, and there I did
plainly hear the dashing of the oares of the boats in the Thames to Arundell
gallery window, which, without it, I could not in the least do, and may, I
believe, be improved to a great height, which I am mighty glad of."

LONGVIL.

They can hear distinctly a league at sea by them already.

SIR NICHOLAS.

Pish, that's nothing. I have made one you may hear eight mile about, and I shall improve it very much more, for there's no stop in art. But of all languages none is heard so far as Greek. Your Ionic dialect of *Oio* does so roll in the sound. I make Sir Formal speak Greek often in it. 50

BRUCE.

This Sir Formal has a great many pretty employments under him.

SIR NICHOLAS.

I doubt not but in three months to improve it so, that from the chief mountain, hill, or eminence in a county a man may be heard round the county. 55

LONGVIL.

This will be above all wonder.

SIR NICHOLAS.

I have thought of this to do the king service. For when I have perfected it, there needs but one parson to preach to a whole county. The king may then take all the church lands into his own hands and serve all England with his chaplains in ordinary. 60

LONGVIL.

This is a most admirable project. But what will become of the rest of the parsons?

SIR NICHOLAS.

It is no matter. Let 'em learn to make woollen cloth and advance the manufacture of the nation, or learn to make nets and improve the fishing trade. It is a fine, sedentary life for those idle fellows in black. 65

BRUCE [*to* Longvil].

These illiterate virtuosos hate all that have relation to learning. 70

LONGVIL [*to* Bruce].

You cannot blame 'em. —But there being no stop in art, you may advance this trumpet so far you may make 'em talk from one nation to another.

---

49. *there's . . . art*] see also line 71; one of the catchwords of members of the Royal Society; another favorite was "*Plus ultra.*"

SIR NICHOLAS.

So I may in time.

BRUCE.

By this princes may converse, treat, congratulate, and   75
condole, without the great charge and trouble of ambassa-
dors.

SIR NICHOLAS.

I hope to effect it. But I wonder Sir Formal is not return'd.
I sent him to fix my telescopes for surveying the moon.

LONGVIL.

Do you believe the moon is an earth as you told us?   80

SIR NICHOLAS.

Believe it! I know it. I shall shortly publish a book of
geography for it. Why, 'tis as big as our earth. I can see all
the mountainous parts, and valleys, and seas, and lakes in
it; nay, the larger sort of animals, as elephants and camels;
but public buildings and ships very easily. I have seen   85
several battles fought there. They have great guns and have
the use of gunpowder. At land they fight with elephants
and castles. I have see 'em.

BRUCE [to Longvil].

No fanatic that has lost his wits in revelation is so mad as
this fool.   90

LONGVIL [to Bruce].

You are mistaken. This is but a faint copy to some originals
among the tribe.

SIR NICHOLAS.

There's now a great monarch who has armies in several
countries in the moon, which we find out because the colors
which we see are all alike. There are a great many states   95
which we take to be confederates against him. He is a very
ambitious prince and aims at universal monarchy, but the
rest of the moon will be too hard for him.

Enter Sir Formal.

SIR FORMAL.

I have fix'd the tubes in the garden. And if we be not

80. an] *Q 2–3;* on *Q 1. Lines 81–88,   copy-text.*
93–98 support this emendation of the

deceived, the great monarch is making an attack upon a   100
town, and they are in very hard service.

SIR NICHOLAS.

'Tis probable. We'll haste to see it. But first do me the
favor to speak two or three Greek verses in this trumpet.

SIR FORMAL.

With all my heart.

Sir Formal speaks some verses out of Homer.

Enter Sir Nicholas' Servant.

SERVANT.

Sir, sir, stand upon your guard! The house is beset by a great   105
rabble of people who threaten to pull you out of it and tear
you in pieces.

SIR NICHOLAS.

O Heav'n, what is the matter?

SERVANT.

Sir, they are ribbon weavers who have been informed that
you are he that invented the engine loom, which has   110
provok'd 'em to rise up in arms, and they are resolv'd to be
reveng'd for't. Listen, sir, you may hear 'em.

SIR NICHOLAS.

O what will become of me! Gentlemen, gentlemen, for
Heav'n's sake do something for me. I protest and vow they
wrong me. I never invented anything of use in my life, as   115
Gad shall mend me, not I.

BRUCE [*aside*].

We shall be beaten for being in such damn'd company, and
faith we shall deserve it.   *A noise without.*

SIR NICHOLAS.

Mercy on me! How loud they are! O gentlemen, what is to
be done?   120

LONGVIL.

Get your guns and pistols charg'd. The rabble, like wild
beasts, are frighted at firearms.

SIR NICHOLAS.

Go, get 'em charg'd quickly.

SIR FORMAL.

Now is the time for me to show my parts. I have another
weapon. Let me alone with them.   125

SIR NICHOLAS.

What weapon, Sir Formal?

SIR FORMAL.

Eloquence, I warrant ye. Let me alone. I'll go out among
'em.

SIR NICHOLAS.

O, 'twill never do. They are very outrageous rogues. What
will become of us?   130

SIR FORMAL.

You know not the charms of oratory. 'Twas my fortune to
be near the Temple stairs when the watermen, who had
drunk too deep of a liquor somewhat stronger than that
which is the scene of their vocation, were stirr'd up into so
popular a heat and fervor that its fury threatened the 135
adjacent Society. The watermen were themselves (as I may
so say) blown into a tempest, when straight I ventur'd in
among th' intemperate crowd, and by the force of rhetoric
dispell'd the barbarity of their overboiling ale and too much
fermented choler, and gently recompos'd their minds into a 140
sedate and quiet temper. And I doubt not but to have the
same effect upon these.

SIR NICHOLAS.

Quickly then dispatch. Tell 'em I am innocent. I never
invented anything in my life. Go, go quickly.   *Exeunt.*

[V.iii]

The scene, the street; a great rabble of people together and Snarl, *etc.*

SNARL.

Whatever they say, this Sir Nicholas and one Sir Formal
that's with him invented the engine loom, to the confusion
of the ribbon weavers. (*Aside.*) I shall be sufficiently reveng'd
on the rogues now.

FIRST WEAVER.

O villains! We'll maul 'em. Are these the tricks of a   5
vertoso? Have they studied these fourteen years for this?

136–137. were themselves (. . .)   were blown *Q 3.*
blown] *Q 1–2;* themselves (. . . .)

[V.iii]
  6. *vertoso*] This misspelling in all three editions is probably meant to
indicate mispronunciation by the ribbon weavers.

SNARL.

Yes, for much less. The truth is 'tis a burning shame that
poor men shou'd be ruin'd by such fellows, in sadness, 'tis.

SECOND WEAVER.

I never thought these vertosos would do anything but
mischief, for my part.   10

THIRD WEAVER.

Where are the rogues? —Come out of your den.

ALL.

Come out. Where are the vertosos here?

FIRST WEAVER.

Break open the house. Open the door, or we'll demolish—

PORTER (*within*).

What would you have? Stand off!

FIRST WEAVER.

What would you have, you son of a whore—the engine and   15
the rogues that invented it!

PORTER (*within*).

Here's no engine, no rogues, nor inventors neither.

Enter Sir Formal.

SIR FORMAL [*aside*].

Now will I try my eloquence. —Come, gentlemen, what
is it you would have? What is the fountain of your dis-
contents? (Now for the power of oratory!) Come, come,   20
come—

FIRST WEAVER.

Here's one of the rascals. Take him amongst you.

SIR FORMAL.

Why, gentlemen—

SECOND WEAVER.

Tear him in pieces.

SIR FORMAL.

I say, gentlemen—   25

THIRD WEAVER.

Cut off his ears.

FIRST WEAVER.

Take him and hang him upon the next sign.

SIR FORMAL.

I beseech you.

ALL.

Ay, hang him up quickly.

SIR FORMAL.

Hold! Hold! Shall I not speak?   30

SECOND WEAVER.

Yes, if you can after you are hang'd.

SIR FORMAL.

Why, gentlemen, I am of your side. If you commit this
rash outrage, you will be soundly punish'd upon a *Quare
fremuerunt gentes—*

SOME.

Let him speak.   35

OTHERS.

No, he shall not speak. Hang him.

FIRST WEAVER.

Hold, neighbors and friends, let's hear him. He may perhaps
discover something of this business.

ALL

Let him speak.

SIR FORMAL.

By what occasion or accident this unheard-of torrent of   40
tempestuous rage was thus inflam'd, I very much ignore.
But let it not be said that Englishmen, good commonwealth's
men, and sober, discreet ribbon weavers should be thus
hurried by the rapid force of the too dangerous whirlwind
or hurricane of passion.   45

FIRST WEAVER.

He speaks notably.

SECOND WEAVER.

He's a well-spoken man, truly.

SIR FORMAL.

Of passion, I say, which with its sudden and, alas, too
violent circumgyrations does too often shipwreck those that
are agitated by it, while it turns them into such giddy con-   50
fusion that they can no longer trim the sails of reason or
steer by the compass of judgment.

33–34. *Quare . . . gentes*] the opening words of Psalm 2:1, according to the
Vulgate text; paraphrased in Acts 4:25, as "Why did the heathen rage and
the people consider a vain thing."

FIRST WEAVER.

His tongue's well hung, but I know not what he means by all this stuff.

SIR FORMAL.

I say, gentlemen.   55

SECOND WEAVER.

Pox on you, you shall say no more. What's this to the invention of the loom?

THIRD WEAVER.

This is one of the inventors. Hang him. Where's t' other? Break open the house.

Enter Sir Nicholas, Bruce, *and* Longvil *above.*

SIR FORMAL.

Do but hear me!   60

FIRST WEAVER.

No, rascal, we will not hear you.
                    They beat him, kick him, and fling oranges at him.

SIR FORMAL.

All this I can bear, if you will but hear me, gentlemen. I am a person—

SECOND WEAVER.

A person—a rogue, a villain, a damn'd vertoso! A person!

SIR FORMAL.

I say, gentlemen, I am a person—   65

FIRST WEAVER.

Pox on you. We'll use you like a dog, sir.

SIR FORMAL.

Quo usque tandem effrenata jactabit audacia? This is a barbarity which Scythians would blush at.

FIRST WEAVER.

Scythians! What a pox, does he call us names? Take him and hang him up.   70

---

69. call] *Q2–3;* calls *Q1. Q1's* "*does he calls*" *may possibly be meant to indicate the ribbon weaver's poor* *grammar, but misuse of verbs is employed nowhere else in this scene.*

---

67. *Quo . . . audacia?*] a conflation of the first two and last three words in the first sentence of Cicero's first oration against Catiline: "How long . . . will your unbridled audacity vaunt itself?"

SIR NICHOLAS.

  I see Sir Formal's oratory cannot prevail. What shall I do?

FIRST WEAVER.

  O there he is. —Come down, or we'll fetch you down, and
  your engine too.

LONGVIL.

  Nay, then 'tis time to sally out.

BRUCE.

  Give us pistols quickly.   75

SIR NICHOLAS.

  Hear me, gentlemen, I never invented an engine in my life.
  As Gad shall sa' me, you do me wrong. I never invented so
  much as an engine to pare cream cheese with. We virtuosos
  never find out anything of use, 'tis not our way.

FIRST WEAVER.

  Hang your way. You are a damn'd, lying vertoso. —Break   80
  open the door quickly.

          Enter Longvil *and* Bruce *below with pistols, servants.*

BRUCE.

  Where are these dogs?

                              Discharge their pistols; all run out.

SIR FORMAL.

  Murder! Murder!   *Falls down.*

          Enter Sir Nicholas *creeping out with a blunderbuss.*

SIR NICHOLAS.

  Where are these rogues?

LONGVIL [*to a footman*].

  Sirrah, go and call the guard lest they should rally again.   85
                                                  [*Servant exits.*]

BRUCE.

  Sir Formal is shot, and all the rabble is escap'd unhurt.

SIR NICHOLAS.

  O my friend! Sir Formal, Sir Formal!

SIR FORMAL.

  I am alive, Sir Nicholas, but surely I am shot.

SIR NICHOLAS.

  Let's search. Here is no hole in your clothes.

85. lest] *Q1;* least *Q2–3.*

SIR FORMAL.

> Hum. I find no blood. Truly I did opine that I was shot— 90
> but I am exceedingly beaten and bruised. Though there be
> no discretion, I have suffered much confusion.

SIR NICHOLAS.

> I see your oratory could not prevail.

SIR FORMAL.

> No, no, these barbarians understand not eloquence. But I
> must go in and recover this disorder.   *Exit.* 95

BRUCE [*to* Longvil].

> Let's take this opportunity to get rid of the Virtuoso and go
> to the masquerade.

> [*Enter* Footman.]

FOOTMAN.

> Sir, the guard was coming to suppress the tumult ere I went.
> They seiz'd some of the mutineers and dispers'd the rest.

LONGVIL.

> Now we are safe, sir. We humbly take our leaves till to- 100
> morrow.   *Exeunt* Longvil *and* Bruce.

SIR NICHOLAS.

> Gentlemen, your humble servant. [*To* Porter.] Where
> are my wife and nieces?

PORTER.

> They are gone abroad, sir.

SIR NICHOLAS.

> At this time o' night? Did they go together?   105

PORTER.

> No, sir, my lady went alone.

SIR NICHOLAS.

> And did you let my nieces go out, villain, without your
> lady?

PORTER.

> Sir Formal carried them out.

SIR NICHOLAS [*aside*].

> 'Death! What design is this? They are gone to the masquer- 110
> ade. My wife alone too! I like not this. The story in German
> Street was very suspicious. I shall find out these practices.
>   *Exeunt.*

94. But] *Q1; om. Q2-3.*   95. recover] *Q1;* discover *Q2-3.*

[V.iv]

The scene is a large room with a great number of masqueraders, men and women, in many different habits. Enter Sir Samuel *and* Hazard.

SIR SAMUEL.

Now, Hazard, let's enjoy ourselves. I am never in my element, but when I am adventuring about an *intriguo* or masquerading about business. Now you shall see me show my parts.

HAZARD.

Do. Sir Samuel, you are excellent at these things.   5

SIR SAMUEL.

Nay, if any man outdoes me about this business— Well, no more to be said. Is not mine a very pretty disguise? Ha.

HAZARD.

An admirable one.

SIR SAMUEL.

I have forty of 'em upon *intriguos* and businesses. But now to work. (*To* Clarinda.) Do you know me?   10

CLARINDA.

No, yet methinks you look through your disguise like a foolish fellow I have seen.

SIR SAMUEL.

A foolish fellow! Hey, poop! You were never so much in the wrong in your life, as Gad mend me.

CLARINDA.

I do not think so. A mask might cover deformity, but not   15 folly. You have the very mien of a coxcomb. All the motions of your body declare the weakness of your mind.

SIR SAMUEL.

Pish! What, you are upon the high ropes now. [*Aside.*] Whipstitch, your nose in my breech. Pish, I'll talk no more with her.   20

HAZARD (*to* Miranda).

Do you know me?

MIRANDA.

No, I neither know ye, nor care to know ye.

22. ye . . . ye] *Q1–2;* you . . . you *Q3.*

– 121 –

HAZARD.

They who have so little curiosity have less pleasure.

MIRANDA.

I guess your inside to be no better than your outside.

HAZARD.

Try 'em both, and you'll be of another opinion.   25

MIRANDA.

The conviction's not worth the trial.

LADY GIMCRACK [aside].

I wonder which is Hazard. But my business is not with him.

SIR SAMUEL.

These are very angry ladies, Hazard. Just now we met two
were very kind to us. Pretty rogues, they had delicate hands,
arms, and necks, and they were women of quality, I'm sure   30
by their linen.

HAZARD.

That's no rule, for whores wear as good linen as honest
women. Fine clothes and good linen are the working tools
of their trade.

SIR SAMUEL.

But I know by their wit and repartees they were fine   35
persons. I am confident my woman knows me and has a
kindness for me.

HAZARD.

Methought they seem'd to be rank strumpets.

SIR SAMUEL.

Prithee hold thy peace. *Tace* is Latin for a candle. I am used
to these intrigues and businesses.   40

Enter Longvil *and* Bruce *in their own clothes, masked.*

CLARINDA [to Miranda].

Longvil and Bruce! Let's watch them and see where they'll
direct themselves.

MIRANDA [to Clarinda].

Like right-bred men o' th' town, I warrant, upon the next
they light on.

SIR SAMUEL.

'Ods my life, I ha' lost my lac'd handkerchief.   45

40. intrigues] *Q1–2; intrigos Q3.*

HAZARD.

    'Death! I ha' lost mine too. 'Heart! All my money's gone.

SIR SAMUEL.

    Ha! Money! What a pox, mine's all flown too. Whip slap-
    dash—

HAZARD.

    Whip slapdash! A pox o' your women of quality; they are
    flown too. Whip slapdash! But you have been us'd to such   50
    intriguos and businesses—

SIR SAMUEL.

    I durst ha' sworn I could not be deceiv'd. Though I ha'
    been often serv'd so by vizard masks in the pit (they are
    mightily giv'n to't), we men of adventure must bear this.
    Come, no more to be said. Come, 'tis well it's no worse.   55
    Come.

LONGVIL.

    This is a fine, civil assembly, truly. The knight has great
    conveniences of coaches and retiring rooms.

BRUCE.

    It is a very rank ball; there's like to be very much fornication
    committed tonight.   60

LONGVIL.

    A masquerade's good for nothing else but to hide blushes
    and bring bashful people together who are asham'd to sin
    barefac'd. There's a lady hovering about you and longs to
    pickeer with you.

                               Lady Gimcrack *stares on* Bruce.

BRUCE.

    O that it were Clarinda in a good mind!   65

LONGVIL.

    I wish it be not Miranda in a bad one. Her shape's like
    hers.

SIR SAMUEL.

    Come, fiddles, be ready. —Shall I wait on you in a dance
    about business—

---

    64. *pickeer*] to skirmish playfully or amorously; to dally, flirt. (*OED*
quotes this passage.)

the bourée— *Takes out* Clarinda. 70

They dance; Sir Samuel leaves her; she takes in another.

CLARINDA.

A courante.

BRUCE.

May I not have the honor to know who you are?

LADY GIMCRACK.

'Tis sufficient to tell you I am one you have no ill wishes to
and would not tell you this but in a mask.

BRUCE [*aside*].

She's finely shap'd and by her jewels a woman of some 75
condition. —Come, off with this cloud to a good face and
ornament to a bad one.

LADY GIMCRACK.

No, but if you will withdraw into another room, I'll let you
know more of my mind, though not of my face.

BRUCE.

The temptation is too strong to be resisted. Let's steal off. 80

They steal out.

Entry of scaramouches and clowns. Dance.

SIR SAMUEL.

Very fine, I swear, very fine. [*Aside.*] Where the devil's
this Miranda? I cannot find her out for my life.

CLARINDA [*to* Miranda].

Did you not see Bruce steal off with a lady?

MIRANDA [*to* Clarinda].

Yes, and cannot bear it. I am so foolish; I would I were not.

SIR SAMUEL.

But hold. Who held my sword while I danced? 'Twas a 85
French sword, cost me fifteen pistoles. A curse on him, he's
rubb'd off with—But come, 'tis well it's no worse, yet—

---

70. bourée] boree *Q1–3.*
71. courante] corant *Q1–3.*
74. in a mask] *Q1, 3;* in mask *Q2.*

80.2. *scaramouches*] *scaramonchi Q1;*
scaramouchi Q2–3.
87. with—] *Q1–2;* with it— *Q3.*

---

70. *bourée*] a lively dance from the Auvergne.
71. *courante*] a French or Italian dance with quick running steps.
86. *pistoles*] a name formerly applied to certain foreign gold coins.
87. *rubb'd off*] made off; stolen and disappeared.

LONGVIL [*aside*].

This Bruce stays somewhat long; I like it not. If I could
find out either Clarinda or Miranda here, I should be out
of doubt. —Let me see, who are you?   90

MRS. FIGGUP.

(*She speaks in a poppet's voice.*)
What authority have you to examine me?

LONGVIL.

What have we here, a poppet?

MRS. FIGGUP.

Such a poppet as you'll be glad to change for the player
you keep.

LONGVIL.

You are mistaken. I love the stage too well to keep any of   95
their women, to make 'em proud and insolent and despise
that calling to take up a worse.

MRS. FIGGUP.

Then you are none of the fops I took you for.

Enter Bruce and Lady Gimcrack.

BRUCE.

I can never rest till I know who has oblig'd me.

LADY GIMCRACK.

Since you are so importunate, I'll give you a note will 100
discover it, if you'll give me your honor not to open it till the
masquerade be done.

BRUCE.

Upon my honor, I will not.

LADY GIMCRACK.

Now show yourself a man of honor.

BRUCE.

Gad, I think I have already.   105

Enter Sir Formal in Scaramouche's habit.

CLARINDA.

Yonder's Sir Formal. You have your cue, Betty.

BETTY.

I warrant you, madam.   (*To* Sir Formal.)   You see I am as
good as my word.

---

91. S.D. *poppet's voice*] puppet's voice, i.e., high and squeaky.

SIR FORMAL [*aside*].

> 'Tis she by her bracelet and pendants. —Madam, had not
> some disaster intervened, I had sooner kiss'd your hands. 110
> But of that, more anon.

Enter Lady Gimcrack *in another disguise.*

LADY GIMCRACK [*aside*].

> Now for the rest of my plot. I shall disappoint these young
> sluts, or make mischief enough.

> *Exeunt* Longvil *and* Lady Gimcrack.

Enter Snarl, *barefac'd.*

MIRANDA [*to* Clarinda].

> Did you not see Longvil steal out with a woman?

CLARINDA [*to* Miranda].

> Too well. Our lovers are well match'd.   115

SNARL.

> In sadness, I think Bedlam's broke loose and come hither.
> What a company of antic puppies are here! Pox on 'em all.
> But where is this Figgup? By the mass, I'll not suffer her to
> go to these schools of bawdry. In sadness, she'll be too apt a
> scholar I am afraid.   120

SIR SAMUEL.

> Hey Snarl! What, do you come to a masquerade barefac'd?

SNARL.

> Yes, that I do, nor am I asham'd of my face as rogues and
> whores are. Whose fool are you?

CLARINDA.

> Sir, will you please to dance?

SNARL.

> No indeed won't I. I thank God I am not such a coxcomb 125
> yet, in sadness. What do you find in my face to think me
> such an owl?

MIRANDA.

> What do you come for then?

SNARL.

> Why to find one that should be wiser than to be here, by
> the mass.   130

114. Did you not] *Q1;* Did not you
Q2–3.

MRS. FIGGUP [*aside*].

He means me. I shall be undone.

CLARINDA.

Whom do you mean? She that was in the woodhole?

MIRANDA.

She that was discover'd in German Street?

SNARL [*aside*].

'Ounds! I shall be a byword all over the town, in sadness.

Enter Sir Nicholas.

SIR NICHOLAS [*aside*].

My uncle here!   135

CLARINDA.

Is it she you look for?

SNARL.

What pert, sniveling, squeaking baggages are you? Here's a squealing with you, with a pox to you!

HAZARD [*to* Sir Samuel].

To him, Sir Samuel.

SIR SAMUEL (*in a squeaking tone*).

Sir, let me ask you one civil question.   140

SNARL (*mocking him*).

What civil question would you ask now?

SIR SAMUEL.

Were not you with a lady in German Street pull'd out by the heels today?

SNARL.

'Ounds! What rogue art thou? I could find in my heart to beat thee most exorbitantly.   145

HAZARD.

Your landlady in German Street is a schoolmistress, is she not, sir?

SNARL [*aside*].

O my shame comes upon me! —In sadness, you are all a company of squealing coxcombs. Would you were all eunuchs, by the mass, that you might always keep your 150 treble voices.

FIRST BULLY.

What, was this virtuous gentleman taken with a whore?

SECOND BULLY.

Sir, do you very much delight in birch?

SIR SAMUEL.

Yes, for mortification sake. He's a great doer of penance.

HAZARD.

A fine old gentleman, with grey hairs, to be overtaken!   155

SIR FORMAL.

Truly I am sorry a person of your gravity should so expose
your discretion.

SNARL.

What damn'd antic rascal's this!   *Kicks him.*

SIR FORMAL.

As Gad mend me, it was uncivil. —But madam, we will
retire, if you please.   160

SNARL.

What a devil, shall I be overset with rogues and fools
here?

FIRST BULLY.

Damn rogues and fools.

SNARL.

So I say, in sadness. The men are all rogues and fools, and
the women all strumpets, by the mass, or which are ten times   165
worse scandalous honest women. In sadness, it is a shame
such bawdy doings should be suffered in a civil nation.
My heart bleeds for't, by the mass. It was not so in the last
age. Why, what do I talk with a company of owls for? I
come to find one whom I'll never seek again if she will not   170
appear now.

MRS. FIGGUP.

O buddy, I am here, but I was afraid you'd be anger'd.

SNARL.

In sadness, I wonder you are not asham'd to come to
these vicious, scandalous, bawdy places. Come away, for
shame.   *Exeunt* Snarl *and* Mrs. Figgup.   175

Enter Longvil and Lady Gimcrack.

LONGVIL.

I never yet knew one so free of her body and so nice of

172. be anger'd] be an anger'd
Q1–3.

her face before. Shall I know no more of you?

LADY GIMCRACK.

Since you will have it so, there's a note will inform you
more. But upon your honor you must not open it till the
masquerade be over.   180

LONGVIL.

I will not.

SIR NICHOLAS.

My dear, I wonder'd I could not see you before.

LADY GIMCRACK.

O Hazard, have I found thee? This is good luck, my
dear.

SIR NICHOLAS [aside].

O infamous, damn'd woman!   185

LADY GIMCRACK.

It makes me break my spleen almost to think what an
ass we made of Sir Nicholas today.

SIR NICHOLAS.

Ay, so it does mine. Ha-ha-ha. [Aside.] A curse on
womankind!

LADY GIMCRACK.

He, poor fool, believes us all this while to be as innocent. 190
Now shall you have free liberty to come home to me.

SIR NICHOLAS [revealing himself to her].

Shall he so, madam?   Lady Gimcrack shrieks out.

SIR SAMUEL.

What's here? One offering violence to a lady!

HAZARD.

Who? This my Lady Gimcrack?

LADY GIMCRACK [to Hazard].

It is my husband. For Heaven's sake, keep him here till I 195
run home.   Exit Lady Gimcrack.

HAZARD.

Villain! How dare you abuse a lady!   Kicks him.

SIR NICHOLAS.

It's no matter for that, I shall not discover myself.

HAZARD [to Sir Samuel].

It is Sir Nicholas. Now you may lock him up and be
reveng'd of him.   200

200. of] Q 1–2; on Q 3.

SIR SAMUEL.

> No more to be said. —Hey, who waits there? Take this
> fellow and lock him up till I talk with him about business.

SIR NICHOLAS.

> 'Death! What will become of me?

LONGVIL [*aside*].

> I have fix'd upon almost every woman of the masquerade
> and cannot find which is either Clarinda or Miranda.   205

FIRST BULLY.

> 'Ounds you lie.

SECOND BULLY.

> Take that, rascal.

They draw, and all draw. Exeunt all [except Sir Samuel], women shrieking.

SIR SAMUEL.

> These damn'd bully rogues have spoil'd my intrigue. A pox
> on 'em all. The ladies are gone. But I'll find a way to be
> convey'd into Miranda's chamber tonight yet.   210

> > *Exit* Sir Samuel.

[V.v]   *Enter* Longvil, Bruce, *and* Porter.

LONGVIL.

> Is not Sir Nicholas within?

PORTER.

> No, but my lady and the two ladies are come. My lady
> is gone up to my master's closet, and the young ladies are
> in the garden.

BRUCE.

> We come to tell Sir Nicholas we've wholly quell'd the   5
> mutiny and seen the offenders committed.

PORTER.

> He will be within presently.   *Exit.*

LONGVIL.

> I do not see the ladies here. But this was a very strange
> adventure at the masquerade.

BRUCE.

> The circumstances are so like, had I not seen two several   10

[V.v]
0.1.] *scene division om. Q1–3.*

habits, I should believe 'twas the same woman I have a
note to and receiv'd the same injunction not to open it.

LONGVIL.

Let me read your note, and you shall read mine. The
moonlight will serve for that. (*Aside.*) By that means I
may discover something.   15

BRUCE.

Agreed. (*Aside.*) I may perhaps make a discovery.
(*Reads.*) "You see I dare not own my kindness but when
I had something to hide my blushes. I hope you'll use the
conquest like a gentleman.

CLARINDA."   20

LONGVIL.

How! This is to the same effect, subscrib'd by Miranda.
There needs no further argument of your treachery, and
such as I did not think a gentleman could be guilty of.

BRUCE.

'Death! Do you accuse me of treachery, who are yourself
so great a traitor! Draw!   25

LONGVIL.

Are you so nimble? Have at you.   *Fight.*

Enter Clarinda *and* Miranda.

CLARINDA. MIRANDA.

Hold! Hold! Hold! For Heav'n's sake, hold!

CLARINDA.

What means this madness in this place?

BRUCE.

I suppose you guess at the meaning.

LONGVIL.

If not, Miranda can inform you.   30

MIRANDA.

This is absolute distraction, gentlemen.

BRUCE.

You let Longvil know more of your mind, madam, in a
private room at the masquerade tonight.

LONGVIL.

If she did not, this lady was kind enough to you there.

MIRANDA.

What madness is this? I spoke ne'er a word to either of you 35 there.

CLARINDA.

Nor I, Heav'n knows! But we saw each of you steal away with a lady.

BRUCE.

Do you know that hand, madam?

[*Shows note*] *to* Clarinda.

LONGVIL.

Or you this, madam? [*Shows the other note*] *to* Miranda. 40

CLARINDA.

My name subscrib'd!

MIRANDA.

And here is mine!

CLARINDA.

This mischief is too evident. This is my aunt's hand.

MIRANDA.

And this is her character, too. This malice is beyond example, and your baseness, so soon to entertain such 45 thoughts of us.

CLARINDA.

That senseless vanity that makes them think so well of themselves made 'em think so ill of us.

LONGVIL.

O Heaven, what have we done! I beg a thousand pardons for my fault. 50

BRUCE.

Hear but my acknowledgment; on my knees I beg forgiveness for my ill thoughts of so excellent a lady.

CLARINDA.

Be gone, unworthy men, and never see us more.

MIRANDA.

I'll ne'er forgive the man that thus dare injure me.

Exeunt Clarinda *and* Miranda.

LONGVIL.

This damn'd lady has put herself upon us for two women. 55 Let's not leave 'em till we have satisfied them of the occasion of our jealousy.

BRUCE.

Let's follow at a distance.

> Longvil *and* Bruce *follow 'em* [*and exit*].

Enter Clarinda *and* Miranda *and go into an arbor.* [*Enter* Longvil *and* Bruce.]

LONGVIL.

They are gone into that arbor. Let's do an ungenerous
thing for once and listen.   60

BRUCE.

Agreed. We then perhaps may hear what their resentments
are.   [Longvil *and* Bruce *conceal themselves by the arbor.*]

CLARINDA.

I see we must carry ourselves with more reservedness since
men of wit and pleasure are so apt to think ill of our
sex.   65

CLARINDA.

For all this, I love Longvil to that height I cannot be
reserved to him. I can forgive him anything.

MIRANDA.

I love Bruce too, almost to distraction, and could venture
anything but honor for him.

CLARINDA.

I'd lose my life and love a thousand times before my virtue.   70
But our cross love can never meet.

MIRANDA.

The breach was great enough before, but this falsehood
and malice of my lady has made it wider. But hold, we are
overheard!

CLARINDA.

O Heav'n! Here are Longvil and Bruce!   75

> *They run away shrieking.*

LONGVIL.

Our case is plain; we have no hopes of succeeding in our
intended loves. Or if I had, I would not have the body
without the mind.

BRUCE.

A man enjoys as much by a rape as that way. But I am so
pleas'd to find Miranda loves me that I'd not change for any   80
but Clarinda.

LONGVIL.

I have the same opinion of Clarinda's love; and could you
be contented, I would willingly change. Gratitude to her
will move my heart more than Miranda's charms with her
aversion can.   85

BRUCE.

Since our affections will not thrive in the soil we had plac'd
them in, we must transplant them.

LONGVIL.

Love, like the sunbeams, will not warm much unless
reflected back again. It is resolv'd it shall be so.

BRUCE.

Let's follow them now; and while the metal's hot, 'twill take   90
a bent the easier.   *Exeunt.*

[V.vi]   *Enter* Sir Nicholas, Lady Gimcrack.

SIR NICHOLAS.

Infamous, vile woman, I'll be reveng'd on all your lewdness.

LADY GIMCRACK.

I have broken open your closet, and here are all your
letters from your several whores. And do you think I'll
bear your falsehood without revenge?

SIR NICHOLAS.

Be gone out of my doors. I cast you from me, and I have   5
here another mistress of this house. —Come in.

Enter Mrs. Flirt.

To you I give possession of all here, madam.   [*To* Lady
Gimcrack.]   Out of my doors.

LADY GIMCRACK.

Is this one of the creatures you converse with about philosophical matters! Fare ye well. I have, thanks to my friends,   10
a settlement for separate maintenance, and I have provided
for myself, too, a worthy gentleman. —Come in, sir. —He
will defend my person and my honor.

Enter Hazard.

SIR NICHOLAS.

Whoe'er shall make such settlements hereafter, may they

0.1.] *Scena ultima Q1–3.*   10. ye] *Q1–2;* you *Q3.*

---

be plagu'd as I am. —Vile creature.   15

LADY GIMCRACK.

Sir, I shall publish your letters into bargain and send 'em
to Gresham College. Then you'll be more despis'd than
now you are there.

SIR NICHOLAS [aside].

O misfortune! That will be worse than all the miseries can
happen to me. —Hold, madam, I have thought on't; and to   20
show how much I can be a philosopher, I am content it
should be a drawn battle betwixt us. Do you forgive, and
you shall find that I can do so too.

Enter Steward.

STEWARD.

O sir, I bring you the most unfortunate news that e'er you
heard.   25

SIR NICHOLAS.

More crosses still!

STEWARD.

Several engineers, glassmakers, and other people you have
dealt with for experiments have brought executions and
extents and seiz'd on all your estate in the country.

LADY GIMCRACK.

'Tis very well. You were all this while bottling of air and   30
studying spiders and glowworms, stinking fish, and rotten
wood.

SIR NICHOLAS.

This last affliction is too great to bear. But I am resolv'd to
forgive thee, my dear, and be a good husband, and redeem
all.   35

LADY GIMCRACK.

No, sir, I thank you. My settlement is without incumbrance,
and I'll preserve it without you, which you are the greatest
a woman can have.

Enter Sir Formal *and* Betty.

---

28. *executions*] judicial writs by which an officer is empowered to carry a
judgment into effect.

29. *extents*] writs to recover judgments, under which the lands, goods,
and person of the debtor may all be seized to secure payment.

37–38. *which . . . have.*] i.e., Sir Nicholas is the greatest incumbrance
Lady Gimcrack can have.

SIR FORMAL.

Sir, I humbly implore your pardon for a crime which love,
which was too strong for my resistance, caused in me.   40

SIR NICHOLAS.

What do you mean?

SIR FORMAL.

I have married Clarinda. The pretty creature had an odd
fancy to be married in masquerade. I hope you'll pardon it.
Love is not in our power.

SIR NICHOLAS.

O Heav'n, this is to add to all the rest! —No, base man, I   45
never will forgive it.

BETTY (*unmasks*).

Sir, you may if you please, and he too. Consider, sir, love
is not in our power.

SIR FORMAL.

I am amaz'd! I am struck dumb! I ne'er shall speak again!

SIR NICHOLAS.

I am sorry for you, Sir Formal, but I have greater sorrows   50
of my own. Yet I have my Uncle Snarl in reserve. I'll try
his bounty. O here he is.

Enter Snarl *and* Mrs. Figgup.

SNARL.

Here! Where is this coxcomb, nephew, this virtuoso? I was
with a whore in German Street, was I? —And your ladyship reproach'd me too. She is your aunt, in sadness.   55

SIR NICHOLAS.

How, sir! What do you mean?

SNARL.

Mean, why what should I mean? She is my wife; I am
married to her.

MRS. FIGGUP.

Yes, sir, we are married, I assure you.

SIR NICHOLAS [*aside*].

O, this is worst of all. I have lost all hopes of his estate, for   60
which I've so long suffer'd all his frowardness.

Enter Longvil, Bruce, Clarinda, Miranda.

LADY GIMCRACK [*aside*].

O Heav'n! Are they so soon come to a right understanding?

I am undone. Curse on 'em!

SNARL.

O gentlemen, that foolish virtuoso and that wordy puppy
Sir Formal said I was taken with a whore in German   65
Street. This is the lady, and she's my wife.

HAZARD.

Be pleas'd to give Sir Formal joy. He is married to Mrs.
Betty, too.

SIR FORMAL.

Upon my sincerity, madam, it was very uncivilly done to
slur your maid upon me in your stead. But I must rest   70
contented; no more to be said.

CLARINDA.

Betty, I wish thee joy. —Sir Formal, she's as good a gentle-
woman as you a gentleman.

SNARL.

I thought my foolish, flashy orator would be catch'd at
last. Ha-ha-ha. What, marry a chambermaid!   75

SIR FORMAL.

But, sir, I have not married a strumpet as you have.

LONGVIL.

How! Is this virtuous gentleman of the last age so overtaken?

BRUCE.

Did gentlemen and men of honor marry whores in the last
age?   80

SNARL.

In sadness, they have much ado to avoid it in this. If I have
married one, she is my own; and I had better marry my
own than another man's, by the mass, as 'tis fifty to one I
should if I had married elsewhere, in sadness.

SIR NICHOLAS [aside].

I have yet a reserve. —Nieces, my land in the country is   85
extended, and my goods are seiz'd on. The money which
I have of yours will redeem all, and I will account with
you.

CLARINDA.

Sir, I can do nothing but by my guardian's consent, and I
have chosen Mr. Longvil for mine.   90

MIRANDA.

And Mr. Bruce has undertaken the protection of my
fortune.

SIR NICHOLAS [*aside*].

'Death! Now all my hopes are cut off. I thought to have
made a good sum of money of my nieces. —Was this the
philosophy you came for, gentlemen?   95

Enter two Porters *with* Sir Samuel *in a chest.*

How now! Whom have we here?

PORTER.

Sir, here is a chest of goods directed to Mrs. Miranda, and
we were commanded to bring it to her.

MIRANDA.

For me? Set it down there.

PORTER.

Shall we not carry it into your chamber, madam?   100

MIRANDA.

No. There's something for you. Be gone.   *Exeunt* Porters.

CLARINDA.

It stands in the way. —Footmen, set it upon one end.
They offer to turn Sir Samuel *with his head down.*

SIR SAMUEL.

Hold, hold! Murder, murder!

SIR NICHOLAS.

How's this? Some rogue and thief. —Pull him out.
[*Footmen pull* Sir Samuel *out.*]

SIR SAMUEL.

Rogue and thief! I scorn your words.   105

SNARL.

An antic coxcomb! I have seen a baboon with more
common sense.

SIR SAMUEL.

I came hither to my mistress Miranda and would marry her
about this business.

BRUCE.

You must ask my leave. She has chosen me for her guardian, 110
and I will cut your throat if you attempt to make love to
her any more.

SIR SAMUEL.

And do you own what he says, madam?

MIRANDA.

I must be rul'd by my guardian.

SIR SAMUEL.

Why then, I have been kick'd, beaten, pumped, and 115
toss'd in a blanket, and so forth, to no purpose. I am
unfortunate in this *intriguo*. But no more to be said. Come,
'tis well it's no worse yet.

SIR NICHOLAS.

Sure, Sir Formal, you'll not deny me that.

SIR FORMAL.

Truly I opine it not reasonable for one who has married 120
one with nothing to be security for another.

SIR NICHOLAS.

That I should know men no better! I would I had studied
mankind instead of spiders and insects. —Sure, my dear,
thou wilt not leave me!

LADY GIMCRACK.

I am resolv'd to part this moment.   125

SIR NICHOLAS.

Well, I have something left yet; and here's one loves me—
she has told me so a thousand times.

MRS. FLIRT.

Sir, trust not to that, for women of my profession love men
but as far as their money goes.

SIR NICHOLAS.

Am I deserted by all? Well, now 'tis time to study for use. I 130
will presently find out the philosopher's stone. I had like to
have gotten it last year but that I wanted May dew, being a
dry season.

LONGVIL.

I hope, ladies, since you have put your estates into our
hands, you'll let us dispose of your persons.   135

MIRANDA.

You must have time to leave off your old love before you
put on new.

CLARINDA.

Nothing but time can fit it to you.

132. being] *Q 1–2;* it being *Q 3.*

BRUCE.

    You have given us hope, and we must live on that awhile.
And sure 'twill not be long that we shall live upon that 140
slender diet, for—

        "If love can once a lady's outworks win,
        It soon will master all that is within."

Exeunt omnes.

---

143. S.D. *Exeunt omnes*] *Q 3; Exeunt
Q 1–2.*

EPILOGUE

Now you who think you're judges of the pit,
Who never but in finding faults show wit,
Who to your dear dull selves are kind alone,
And ne'er reflect on follies of your own:
Our poet can from you no mercy find,   5
Who savage are to all but your own kind.
Nay, on the stage if some of those appear,
Though ne'er so like yourselves, you hate 'em there,
As the whole herd falls on a wounded deer.
But of those ladies he despairs today   10
Who love a dull, romantic, whining play,
Where poor, frail woman's made a deity
With senseless, amorous idolatry,
And sniveling heroes sigh, and pine, and cry.
Though singly they beat armies and huff kings,   15
Rant at the gods, and do impossible things;
Though they can laugh at danger, blood, and wounds;
Yet if the dame once chides, the milksop hero swoons.
These doughty things nor manners have nor wit;
We ne'er saw hero fit to drink with yet.   20
But hold, I hear some say among the rest
This play is not well-bred nor yet well-dressed.
Such plays the women's poets can write best;
They differ from the men's you must allow,
As women's tailors, women's poets too.   25
But know, good breeding shows its excellence
Not in small, trifling forms but in good sense.
Yet, ladies, to stage fools some favor show,
Since off the stage some fops you can allow.
Few of the sex's happy favorites yet   30
Have been the most remarkable for wit.
Sure you must like copies of such as these,
If the original coxcombs can so please.
But to the men of wit our poet flies
And makes his fops to them a sacrifice.   35
You know the pangs and many laboring throws

6. savage] *Q 1–2;* salvage *Q 3.*

By which your brains their perfect births disclose.
You can the faults and excellencies find;
Pass by the one, and be to th' other kind.
By you he is resolv'd to stand or fall;   40
Whate'er's his doom he'll not repine at all.
And if this birth should want its perfect shape
And cannot by your care its death escape,
Th' abortive issue came before its day,
And th' poet has miscarried of a play.   45

FINIS

Appendix

Chronology

Approximate years are indicated by *, occurrences in doubt by (?).

Political and Literary Events   *Life and Works of Thomas Shadwell*

1631
John Dryden born.

1633
Samuel Pepys born.

1635
Sir George Etherege born.*

1640
Aphra Behn born.*

1641
William Wycherley born.*

1642
First Civil War began (ended 1646).   Born in Norfolk of a Royalist
Theaters closed by Parliament.   family.*

1648
Second Civil War.

1649
Execution of Charles I.

1650
Jeremy Collier born.

1651
Hobbes' *Leviathan* published.

1652
First Dutch War began (ended 1654).
Thomas Otway born.

1653
Nathaniel Lee born.*

1656

D'Avenant's *THE SIEGE OF RHODES* performed at Rutland House.

Matriculated on December 17 at Gonville and Caius College, Cambridge.

1657

John Dennis born.

1658

Death of Oliver Cromwell.

D'Avenant's *THE CRUELTY OF THE SPANIARDS IN PERU* performed at the Cockpit.

Became a member of the Middle Temple on July 7.

1660

Restoration of Charles II.

Theatrical patents granted to Thomas Killigrew and Sir William D'Avenant, authorizing them to form, respectively, the King's and the Duke of York's Companies.

Pepys began his diary.

1661

Cowley's *THE CUTTER OF COLEMAN STREET*.

D'Avenant's *THE SIEGE OF RHODES* (expanded to two parts).

1662

Charter granted to the Royal Society.

1663

Dryden's *THE WILD GALLANT*.

Tuke's *THE ADVENTURES OF FIVE HOURS*.

Married Ann Gibbs, a member of the Duke's Company, sometime between 1663 and 1667.

1664

Sir John Vanbrugh born.

Dryden's *THE RIVAL LADIES*.

Dryden and Howard's *THE INDIAN QUEEN*.

Etherege's *THE COMICAL REVENGE*.

1665

Second Dutch War began (ended 1667).

Great Plague.

Dryden's *THE INDIAN*

EMPEROR.
Orrery's *MUSTAPHA.*

1666
Fire of London.
Death of James Shirley.

1667
Milton's *Paradise Lost* published.
Sprat's *The History of the Royal Society* published.
Dryden's *SECRET LOVE.*

1668
Death of D'Avenant.
Dryden made Poet Laureate.
Dryden's *An Essay of Dramatic Poesy* published.

Took exception to Dryden's qualified praise of Jonson.
THE SULLEN LOVERS produced very successfully on May 2.

1669
Pepys terminated his diary.
Susannah Centlivre born.

THE ROYAL SHEPHERDESS produced on February 25.

1670
William Congreve born.
Dryden's *THE CONQUEST OF GRANADA*, Part I.

THE HYPOCRITE (?) and *THE HUMORISTS* produced, the latter about December.

1671
Dorset Garden Theatre (Duke's Company) opened.
Colley Cibber born.
Milton's *Paradise Regained* and *Samson Agonistes* published.
Dryden's *THE CONQUEST OF GRANADA*, Part II.
THE REHEARSAL, by the Duke of Buckingham and others.
Wycherley's *LOVE IN A WOOD.*

Eldest son, John, born.

1672
Third Dutch War began (ended 1674).
Joseph Addison born.
Richard Steele born.
Dryden's *MARRIAGE À LA MODE*

THE MISER (adaptation from Molière) produced about January; *EPSOM WELLS* produced in December.

1673

Joined Dryden and Crowne to attack Settle in *Notes and Observations on the Empress of Morocco* (?).

1674

New Drury Lane Theatre (King's Company) opened.
Death of Milton.
Nicholas Rowe born.
Thomas Rymer's *Reflections on Aristotle's Treatise of Poesy* (translation of Rapin) published.

THE TEMPEST, an opera, produced in April; *THE TRIUMPHANT WIDOW*, written in collaboration with the Duke of Newcastle, produced in November.

1675

Dryden's *AURENG-ZEBE*.
Wycherley's *THE COUNTRY WIFE*.*

PSYCHE, an opera with music by Matthew Locke, and *THE LIBERTINE* produced, the latter in June.

1676

Etherege's *THE MAN OF MODE*.
Otway's *DON CARLOS*.
Wycherley's *THE PLAIN DEALER*.

THE VIRTUOSO produced in May.

1677

Rymer's *Tragedies of the Last Age Considered* published.
Behn's *THE ROVER*.
Dryden's *ALL FOR LOVE*.
Lee's *THE RIVAL QUEENS*.

1678

Popish Plot.
George Farquhar born.
Bunyan's *Pilgrim's Progress* (Part I) published.

THE HISTORY OF TIMON OF ATHENS (adaptation from Shakespeare) produced in January; *A TRUE WIDOW* produced about December.

1679

Exclusion Bill introduced.
Death of Thomas Hobbes.
Death of Roger Boyle, Earl of Orrery.
Charles Johnson born.

THE WOMAN CAPTAIN produced about September.

1680

Death of Samuel Butler.
Death of John Wilmot, Earl of Rochester.
Dryden's *THE SPANISH FRIAR*.
Lee's *LUCIUS JUNIUS BRUTUS*.
Otway's *THE ORPHAN*.

Pallbearer at Samuel Butler's funeral.

1681

Charles II dissolved Parliament at Oxford.

Dryden's *Absalom and Achitophel* published.

Tate's adaptation of *KING LEAR*.

1682.

The King's and the Duke of York's Companies merged into the United Company.

Dryden's *The Medal*, *MacFlecknoe*, and *Religio Laici* published.

Otway's *VENICE PRESERVED*.

1683

Rye House Plot.

Death of Thomas Killigrew.

1685

Death of Charles II; accession of James II.

Revocation of the Edict of Nantes.

The Duke of Monmouth's Rebellion.

Death of Otway.

John Gay born.

Crowne's *SIR COURTLY NICE*.

Dryden's *ALBION AND ALBANIUS*.

1687

Death of the Duke of Buckingham.

Dryden's *The Hind and the Panther* published.

Newton's *Principia* published.

1688

The Revolution.

Alexander Pope born.

1689

The War of the League of Augsburg began.

Toleration Act.

Death of Aphra Behn.

Dryden's *DON SEBASTIAN*.

THE LANCASHIRE WITCHES produced about September.

Called the "Sham-Protestant-Poet" by Nat Thompson; Richard Janeway, the Whig publisher, came to his defense.

Aided financially by Sir Charles Sedley.

The Tenth Satyr of Juvenal licensed May 25.

THE SQUIRE OF ALSATIA produced in May; enjoyed an "uninterrupted run of thirteen days together" (Downes, p. 41).

The patent confirming his appointment to the positions of Poet Laureate and Historiographer Royal drawn up, August 29.

Published two congratulatory poems to William and Mary.

BURY FAIR produced about April.

1690

Battle of the Boyne.

Locke's *Two Treatises of Government* and *An Essay Concerning Human Understanding* published.

1691

Death of Etherege.

Langbaine's *An Account of the English Dramatic Poets* published.

1692

Death of Lee.

Tate made Poet Laureate.

1693

George Lillo born.*

Rymer's *A Short View of Tragedy* published.

Congreve's *THE OLD BACHELOR*.

1694.

Death of Queen Mary.

Southerne's *THE FATAL MARRIAGE*.

1695

Groups of actors led by Thomas Betterton leave Drury Lane and establish a new company at Lincoln's Inn Fields.

Congreve's *LOVE FOR LOVE*.

Southerne's *OROONOKO*.

1696

Cibber's *LOVE'S LAST SHIFT*.

Vanbrugh's *THE RELAPSE*.

1697

Treaty of Ryswick ended the War of the League of Augsburg.

Charles Macklin born.

Congreve's *THE MOURNING BRIDE*.

Vanbrugh's *THE PROVOKED WIFE*.

THE AMOROUS BIGOT produced about March; *THE SCOWRERS* produced about December.

Died in London on November 19 or 20; buried at St. Luke's in Chelsea, November 24.

THE VOLUNTEERS produced posthumously the same month, the epilogue "spoken by one in deep mourning."

1698
Collier controversy started with the publication of *A Short View of the Immorality and Profaneness of the English Stage.*

1699
Farquhar's *THE CONSTANT COUPLE.*

1700
Death of Dryden.
Blackmore's *Satire against Wit* published.
Congreve's *THE WAY OF THE WORLD.*

1701
Act of Settlement.
War of the Spanish Succession began (ended 1713).
Death of James II.
Rowe's *TAMERLANE.*
Steele's *THE FUNERAL.*

1702
Death of William III; accession of Anne.
The Daily Courant began publication.
Cibber's *SHE WOULD AND SHE WOULD NOT.*

1703
Death of Samuel Pepys.
Rowe's *THE FAIR PENITENT.*

1704
Capture of Gibraltar; Battle of Blenheim.
Defoe's *The Review* began publication (1704–1713).
Swift's *A Tale of a Tub* and *The Battle of the Books* published.
Cibber's *THE CARELESS HUSBAND.*

1705
Haymarket Theatre opened.
Steele's *THE TENDER HUSBAND.*

1706

Battle of Ramillies.

Farquhar's *THE RECRUITING OFFICER*.

1707

Union of Scotland and England.

Death of Farquhar.

Henry Fielding born.

Farquhar's *THE BEAUX' STRATAGEM*.

1708

Downes' *Roscius Anglicanus* published.

1709

Samuel Johnson born.

Rowe's edition of Shakespeare published.

The Tatler began publication (1709–1711).

Centlivre's *THE BUSY BODY*.

1711

Shaftesbury's *Characteristics* published.

The Spectator began publication (1711–1712).

Pope's *An Essay on Criticism* published.

1713

Treaty of Utrecht ended the War of the Spanish Succession.

Addison's *CATO*.

1714

Death of Anne; accession of George I.

Steele became Governor of Drury Lane.

John Rich assumed management of Lincoln's Inn Fields.

Centlivre's *THE WONDER: A WOMAN KEEPS A SECRET*.

Rowe's *JANE SHORE*.

1715

Jacobite Rebellion.

Death of Tate.

Rowe made Poet Laureate.

Death of Wycherley.

1716

Addison's *THE DRUMMER.*

1717

David Garrick born.

Cibber's *THE NON-JUROR.*

Gay, Pope, and Arbuthnot's *THREE HOURS AFTER MARRIAGE.*

1718

Death of Rowe.

Centlivre's *A BOLD STROKE FOR A WIFE.*

1719

Death of Addison.

Defoe's *Robinson Crusoe* published.

Young's *BUSIRIS, KING OF EGYPT.*

1720

South Sea Bubble.

Samuel Foote born.

Steele suspended from the Governorship of Drury Lane (restored 1721).

Steele's *The Theatre* (periodical) published.

Hughes' *THE SIEGE OF DAMASCUS.*

1721

Walpole became first Minister.

1722

Steele's *THE CONSCIOUS LOVERS.*

1723

Death of Susannah Centlivre.

Death of D'Urfey.

1725

Pope's edition of Shakespeare published.

1726

Death of Jeremy Collier.

Death of Vanbrugh.

Law's *Unlawfulness of Stage Entertainments* published.

Swift's *Gulliver's Travels* published.

1727

Death of George I; accession of George II.

Death of Sir Isaac Newton.

Arthur Murphy born.

1728

Pope's *Dunciad* published.

Cibber's *THE PROVOKED HUSBAND* (expansion of Vanbrugh's fragment *A JOURNEY TO LONDON*).

Gay's *THE BEGGAR'S OPERA*.

1729

Goodman's Fields Theatre opened.

Death of Congreve.

Death of Steele.

Edmund Burke born.

1730

Cibber made Poet Laureate.

Oliver Goldsmith born.

Thomson's *The Seasons* published.

Fielding's *THE AUTHOR'S FARCE; TOM THUMB* (revised as *THE TRAGEDY OF TRAGEDIES*, 1731).

1731

Death of Defoe.

Lillo's *THE LONDON MERCHANT*.

Fielding's *THE GRUB STREET OPERA*.

1732

Covent Garden Theatre opened.

Death of Gay.

George Colman the elder born.

Fielding's *THE COVENT GARDEN TRAGEDY; THE MODERN HUSBAND*.

Charles Johnson's *CAELIA*.

1733
Pope's *An Essay on Man* (Epistles I–III) published (Epistle IV, 1734).

1734
Death of Dennis.
The Prompter began publication (1734–1736).
Theobald's edition of Shakespeare published.
Fielding's *DON QUIXOTE IN ENGLAND*.

1736
Fielding led the "Great Mogul's Company of Comedians" at the Little Theatre in the Haymarket (1736–1737).
Fielding's *PASQUIN*.
Lillo's *THE FATAL CURIOSITY*.

1737
The Stage Licensing Act.
Dodsley's *THE KING AND THE MILLER OF MANSFIELD*.
Fielding's *THE HISTORICAL REGISTER FOR 1736*.